Books by ROBERT LOWELL

Day by Day (1977)
Selected Poems (1976) (Revised edition, 1977)
The Dolphin (1973)
History (1973)
For Lizzie and Harriet (1973)
Notebook (1969) (Revised and expanded edition, 1970)
Prometheus Bound (1969)
The Voyage & other versions of poems by Baudelaire (1969)
Near the Ocean (1967)
The Old Glory (1965)
For the Union Dead (1964)
Imitations (1961)
Phaedra (translation) (1961)
Life Studies (1959)
The Mills of the Kavanaughs (1951)
Lord Weary's Castle (1946)
Land of Unlikeness (1944)

Selected Poems

Portrait of Robert Lowell by Frank Parker, circa 1950

Robert Lowell

SELECTED

POEMS

[REVISED EDITION]

THE NOONDAY PRESS

Farrar, Straus and Giroux

NEW YORK

For Harriet and Sheridan

Copyright © 1944, 1946, 1947, 1950, 1951,
1956, 1959, 1960, 1961, 1962, 1963, 1964,
1965, 1966, 1967, 1968, 1969, 1970, 1973,
1976, 1977 by Robert Lowell,
copyright renewed 1972, 1974, 1975 by Robert Lowell
All rights reserved
First edition, 1976
Revised edition, 1977

Eighteenth printing, 1996

Printed in the United States of America
Published in Canada by HarperCollins*CanadaLtd*
Designed by Guy Fleming

Poems from *Lord Weary's Castle* and *The Mills
of the Kavanaughs* reprinted by permission of
Harcourt Brace Jovanovich, Inc.

Several of the poems in this book have appeared
elsewhere in slightly different versions or
under different titles

Library of Congress Cataloging in Publication Data
Lowell, Robert.   Selected poems.   Includes index.
PS3523.O89A17   1976   811'.5'2   76–2000

Note

MUCH MAKESHIFT—From my last three books, I have chosen possible sequences, rather than atomizing favorite poems out of context. I have a few slight changes here, often simply going back to discarded versions. I have made no changes in anything earlier, except for cuts in three long poems: *The Mills of the Kavanaughs, Thanksgiving's Over*, and four of the five poems in *Near the Ocean*. My verse autobiography sometimes fictionalizes plot and particular.

R.L.

Note to Revised Edition

This edition of my *Selected Poems* is slightly changed from the original (1976) edition: the five poems from *Near the Ocean* are now printed without cuts; and there have been deletions and additions in the *Dolphin* section, and one addition to the *Nineteen Thirties*.

R.L.

April 27, 1977

Contents

F R O M *Life Studies*

LIFE STUDIES

I

II

F R O M *For the Union Dead*

Nineteen Thirties

xiii

Mexico

F R O M *For Lizzie and Harriet*

PART ONE

PART TWO

FROM *The Dolphin*

xvi

[FROM]

Lord Weary's Castle

The Exile's Return

There mounts in squalls a sort of rusty mire,
Not ice, not snow, to leaguer the Hôtel
De Ville, where braced pig-iron dragons grip
The blizzard to their rigor mortis. A bell
Grumbles when the reverberations strip
The thatching from its spire,
The search-guns click and spit and split up timber
And nick the slate roofs on the Holstenwall
Where torn-up tilestones crown the victor. Fall
And winter, spring and summer, guns unlimber
And lumber down the narrow gabled street
Past your gray, sorry and ancestral house
Where the dynamited walnut tree
Shadows a squat, old, wind-torn gate and cows
The Yankee commandant. You will not see
Strutting children or meet
The peg-leg and reproachful chancellor
With a forget-me-not in his button-hole
When the unseasoned liberators roll
Into the Market Square, ground arms before
The Rathaus; but already lily-stands
Burgeon the risen Rhineland, and a rough
Cathedral lifts its eye. Pleasant enough,
Voi ch'entrate, and your life is in your hands.

Listen, the hay-bells tinkle as the cart
Wavers on rubber tires along the tar
And cindered ice below the burlap mill
And ale-wife run. The oxen drool and start
In wonder at the fenders of a car,
And blunder hugely up St. Peter's hill.
These are the undefiled by woman—their
Sorrow is not the sorrow of this world:
King Herod shrieking vengeance at the curled
Up knees of Jesus choking in the air,

A king of speechless clods and infants. Still
The world out-Herods Herod; and the year,
The nineteen-hundred forty-fifth of grace,
Lumbers with losses up the clinkered hill
Of our purgation; and the oxen near
The worn foundations of their resting-place,
The holy manger where their bed is corn
And holly torn for Christmas. If they die,
As Jesus, in the harness, who will mourn?
Lamb of the shepherds, Child, how still you lie.

Colloquy in Black Rock

Here the jack-hammer jabs into the ocean;
My heart, you race and stagger and demand
More blood-gangs for your nigger-brass percussions,
Till I, the stunned machine of your devotion,
Clanging upon this cymbal of a hand,
Am rattled screw and footloose. All discussions

End in the mud-flat detritus of death.
My heart, beat faster, faster. In Black Mud
Hungarian workmen give their blood
For the martyre Stephen, who was stoned to death.

Black Mud, a name to conjure with: O mud
For watermelons gutted to the crust,
Mud for the mole-tide harbor, mud for mouse,
Mud for the armored Diesel fishing tubs that thud
A year and a day to wind and tide; the dust
Is on this skipping heart that shakes my house,

House of our Savior who was hanged till death.
My heart, beat faster, faster. In Black Mud
Stephen the martyre was broken down to blood:
Our ransom is the rubble of his death.

Christ walks on the black water. In Black Mud
Darts the kingfisher. On Corpus Christi, heart,
Over the drum-beat of St. Stephen's choir
I hear him, *Stupor Mundi*, and the mud
Flies from his hunching wings and beak—my heart,
The blue kingfisher dives on you in fire.

The Quaker Graveyard in Nantucket

[FOR WARREN WINSLOW, DEAD AT SEA]

Let man have dominion over the fishes of the sea and the
fowls of the air and the beasts of the whole earth, and every
creeping creature that moveth upon the earth.

I

A brackish reach of shoal off Madaket—
The sea was still breaking violently and night
Had steamed into our North Atlantic Fleet,
When the drowned sailor clutched the drag-net. Light
Flashed from his matted head and marble feet,
He grappled at the net
With the coiled, hurdling muscles of his thighs:
The corpse was bloodless, a botch of reds and whites,
Its open, staring eyes
Were lustreless dead-lights
Or cabin-windows on a stranded hulk
Heavy with sand. We weight the body, close
Its eyes and heave it seaward whence it came,
Where the heel-headed dogfish barks its nose
On Ahab's void and forehead; and the name
Is blocked in yellow chalk.
Sailors, who pitch this portent at the sea
Where dreadnaughts shall confess
Its hell-bent deity,
When you are powerless
To sand-bag this Atlantic bulwark, faced
By the earth-shaker, green, unwearied, chaste
In his steel scales: ask for no Orphean lute
To pluck life back. The guns of the steeled fleet
Recoil and then repeat
The hoarse salute.

Whenever winds are moving and their breath
Heaves at the roped-in bulwarks of this pier,
The terns and sea-gulls tremble at your death
In these home waters. Sailor, can you hear
The Pequod's sea wings, beating landward, fall
Headlong and break on our Atlantic wall
Off 'Sconset, where the yawing S-boats splash
The bellbuoy, with ballooning spinnakers,
As the entangled, screeching mainsheet clears
The blocks: off Madaket, where lubbers lash
The heavy surf and throw their long lead squids
For blue-fish? Sea-gulls blink their heavy lids
Seaward. The winds' wings beat upon the stones,
Cousin, and scream for you and the claws rush
At the sea's throat and wring it in the slush
Of this old Quaker graveyard where the bones
Cry out in the long night for the hurt beast
Bobbing by Ahab's whaleboats in the East.

I I I

All you recovered from Poseidon died
With you, my cousin, and the harrowed brine
Is fruitless on the blue beard of the god,
Stretching beyond us to the castles in Spain,
Nantucket's westward haven. To Cape Cod
Guns, cradled on the tide,
Blast the eelgrass about a waterclock
Of bilge and backwash, roil the salt and sand
Lashing earth's scaffold, rock
Our warships in the hand
Of the great God, where time's contrition blues
Whatever it was these Quaker sailors lost

In the mad scramble of their lives. They died
When time was open-eyed,
Wooden and childish; only bones abide
There, in the nowhere, where their boats were tossed
Sky-high, where mariners had fabled news
Of IS, the whited monster. What it cost
Them is their secret. In the sperm-whale's slick
I see the Quakers drown and hear their cry:
"If God himself had not been on our side,
If God himself had not been on our side,
When the Atlantic rose against us, why,
Then it had swallowed us up quick."

I V

This is the end of the whaleroad and the whale
Who spewed Nantucket bones on the thrashed swell
And stirred the troubled waters to whirlpools
To send the Pequod packing off to hell:
This is the end of them, three-quarters fools,
Snatching at straws to sail
Seaward and seaward on the turntail whale,
Spouting out blood and water as it rolls,
Sick as a dog to these Atlantic shoals:
Clamavimus, O depths. Let the sea-gulls wail

For water, for the deep where the high tide
Mutters to its hurt self, mutters and ebbs.
Waves wallow in their wash, go out and out,
Leave only the death-rattle of the crabs,
The beach increasing, its enormous snout
Sucking the ocean's side.
This is the end of running on the waves;
We are poured out like water. Who will dance

The mast-lashed master of Leviathans
Up from this field of Quakers in their unstoned graves?

V

When the whale's viscera go and the roll
Of its corruption overruns this world
Beyond tree-swept Nantucket and Woods Hole
And Martha's Vineyard, Sailor, will your sword
Whistle and fall and sink into the fat?
In the great ash-pit of Jehoshaphat
The bones cry for the blood of the white whale,
The fat flukes arch and whack about its ears,
The death-lance churns into the sanctuary, tears
The gun-blue swingle, heaving like a flail,
And hacks the coiling life out: it works and drags
And rips the sperm-whale's midriff into rags,
Gobbets of blubber spill to wind and weather,
Sailor, and gulls go round the stoven timbers
Where the morning stars sing out together
And thunder shakes the white surf and dismembers
The red flag hammered in the mast-head. Hide,
Our steel, Jonas Messias, in Thy side.

V I

OUR LADY OF WALSINGHAM

There once the penitents took off their shoes
And then walked barefoot the remaining mile;
And the small trees, a stream and hedgerows file
Slowly along the munching English lane,
Like cows to the old shrine, until you lose
Track of your dragging pain.

9

The stream flows down under the druid tree,
Shiloah's whirlpools gurgle and make glad
The castle of God. Sailor, you were glad
And whistled Sion by that stream. But see:

Our Lady, too small for her canopy,
Sits near the altar. There's no comeliness
At all or charm in that expressionless
Face with its heavy eyelids. As before,
This face, for centuries a memory,
Non est species, neque decor,
Expressionless, expresses God: it goes
Past castled Sion. She knows what God knows,
Not Calvary's Cross nor crib at Bethlehem
Now, and the world shall come to Walsingham.

VII

The empty winds are creaking and the oak
Splatters and splatters on the cenotaph,
The boughs are trembling and a gaff
Bobs on the untimely stroke
Of the greased wash exploding on a shoal-bell
In the old mouth of the Atlantic. It's well;
Atlantic, you are fouled with the blue sailors,
Sea-monsters, upward angel, downward fish:
Unmarried and corroding, spare of flesh
Mart once of supercilious, wing'd clippers,
Atlantic, where your bell-trap guts its spoil
You could cut the brackish winds with a knife
Here in Nantucket, and cast up the time
When the Lord God formed man from the sea's slime
And breathed into his face the breath of life,
And blue-lung'd combers lumbered to the kill.
The Lord survives the rainbow of His will.

In Memory of Arthur Winslow

DEATH FROM CANCER

This Easter, Arthur Winslow, less than dead,
Your people set you up in Phillips' House
To settle off your wrestling with the crab—
The claws drop flesh upon your yachting blouse
Until longshoreman Charon come and stab
Through your adjusted bed
And crush the crab. On Boston Basin, shells
Hit water by the Union Boat Club wharf:
You ponder why the coxes' squeakings dwarf
The *resurrexit dominus* of all the bells.

Grandfather Winslow, look, the swanboats coast
That island in the Public Gardens, where
The bread-stuffed ducks are brooding, where with tub
And strainer the mid-Sunday Irish scare
The sun-struck shallows for the dusky chub
This Easter, and the ghost
Of risen Jesus walks the waves to run
Arthur upon a trumpeting black swan
Beyond Charles River to the Acheron
Where the wide waters and their voyager are one.

Her Irish maids could never spoon out mush
Or orange-juice enough; the body cools
And smiles as a sick child
Who adds up figures, and a hush
Grips at the poised relations sipping sherry
And tracking up the carpets of her four
Room kingdom. On the rigid Charles, in snow,
Charon, the Lubber, clambers from his wherry,
And stops her hideous baby-squawks and yells,
Wit's clownish afterthought. Nothing will go
Again. Even the gelded picador
Baiting the twinned runt bulls
With walrus horns before the Spanish Belles
Is veiled with all the childish bibelots.

Mary Winslow is dead. Out on the Charles
The shells hold water and their oarblades drag,
Littered with captivated ducks, and now
The bell-rope in King's Chapel Tower unsnarls
And bells the bestial cow
From Boston Common; she is dead. But stop,
Neighbor, these pillows prop
Her that her terrified and child's cold eyes
Glass what they're not: our Copley ancestress,
Grandiloquent, square-jowled and worldly-wise,
A Cleopatra in her housewife's dress;
Nothing will go again. The bells cry: "Come,
Come home," the babbling Chapel belfry cries:
"Come, Mary Winslow, come; I bell thee home."

The Drunken Fisherman

Wallowing in this bloody sty,
I cast for fish that pleased my eye
(Truly Jehovah's bow suspends
No pots of gold to weight its ends);
Only the blood-mouthed rainbow trout
Rose to my bait. They flopped about
My canvas creel until the moth
Corrupted its unstable cloth.

A calendar to tell the day;
A handkerchief to wave away
The gnats; a couch unstuffed with storm
Pouching a bottle in one arm;
A whiskey bottle full of worms;
And bedroom slacks: are these fit terms
To mete the worm whose molten rage
Boils in the belly of old age?

Once fishing was a rabbit's foot—
O wind blow cold, O wind blow hot,
Let suns stay in or suns step out:
Life danced a jig on the sperm-whale's spout—
The fisher's fluent and obscene
Catches kept his conscience clean.
Children, the raging memory drools
Over the glory of past pools.

Now the hot river, ebbing, hauls
Its bloody waters into holes;
A grain of sand inside my shoe
Mimics the moon that might undo
Man and Creation too; remorse,
Stinking, has puddled up its source;

Here tantrums thrash to a whale's rage.
This is the pot-hole of old age.

Is there no way to cast my hook
Out of this dynamited brook?
The Fisher's sons must cast about
When shallow waters peter out.
I will catch Christ with a greased worm,
And when the Prince of Darkness stalks
My bloodstream to its Stygian term . . .
On water the Man-Fisher walks.

Between the Porch and the Altar

MOTHER AND SON

Meeting his mother makes him lose ten years,
Or is it twenty? Time, no doubt, has ears
That listen to the swallowed serpent, wound
Into its bowels, but he thinks no sound
Is possible before her, he thinks the past
Is settled. It is honest to hold fast
Merely to what one sees with one's own eyes
When the red velvet curves and haunches rise
To blot him from the pretty driftwood fire's
Façade of welcome. Then the son retires
Into the sack and selfhood of the boy
Who clawed through fallen houses of his Troy,
Homely and human only when the flames
Crackle in recollection. Nothing shames
Him more than this uncoiling, counterfeit
Body presented as an idol. It
Is something in a circus, big as life,
The painted dragon, a mother and a wife
With flat glass eyes pushed at him on a stick;
The human mover crawls to make them click.
The forehead of her father's portrait peels
With rosy dryness, and the schoolboy kneels
To ask the benediction of the hand,
Lifted as though to motion him to stand,
Dangling its watch-chain on the Holy Book—
A little golden snake that mouths a hook.

ADAM AND EVE

The farmer sizzles on his shaft all day.
He is content and centuries away
From white-hot Concord, and he stands on guard.
Or is he melting down like sculptured lard?
His hand is crisp and steady on the plough.
I quarreled with you, but am happy now
To while away my life for your unrest
Of terror. Never to have lived is best;
Man tasted Eve with death. I taste my wife
And children while I hold your hands. I knife
Their names into this elm. What is exempt?
I eye the statue with an awed contempt
And see the puritanical façade
Of the white church that Irish exiles made
For Patrick—that Colonial from Rome
Had magicked the charmed serpents from their home,
As though he were the Piper. Will his breath
Scorch the red dragon of my nerves to death?
By sundown we are on a shore. You walk
A little way before me and I talk,
Half to myself and half aloud. They lied,
My cold-eyed seedy fathers when they died,
Or rather threw their lives away, to fix
Sterile, forbidding nameplates on the bricks
Above a kettle. Jesus rest their souls!
You cry for help. Your market-basket rolls
With all its baking apples in the lake.

You watch the whorish slither of a snake
That chokes a duckling. When we try to kiss,
Our eyes are slits and cringing, and we hiss;
Scales glitter on our bodies as we fall.
The Farmer melts upon his pedestal.

III

KATHERINE'S DREAM

It must have been a Friday. I could hear
The top-floor typist's thunder and the beer
That you had brought in cases hurt my head;
I'd sent the pillows flying from my bed,
I hugged my knees together and I gasped.
The dangling telephone receiver rasped
Like someone in a dream who cannot stop
For breath or logic till his victim drop
To darkness and the sheets. I must have slept,
But still could hear my father who had kept
Your guilty presents but cut off my hair.
He whispers that he really doesn't care
If I am your kept woman all my life,
Or ruin your two children and your wife;
But my dishonor makes him drink. Of course
I'll tell the court the truth for his divorce.
I walk through snow into St. Patrick's yard.
Black nuns with glasses smile and stand on guard
Before a bulkhead in a bank of snow,
Whose charred doors open, as good people go
Inside by twos to the confessor. One

17

Must have a friend to enter there, but none
Is friendless in this crowd, and the nuns smile.
I stand aside and marvel; for a while
The winter sun is pleasant and it warms
My heart with love for others, but the swarms
Of penitents have dwindled. I begin
To cry and ask God's pardon of our sin.
Where are you? You were with me and are gone.
All the forgiven couples hurry on
To dinner and their nights, and none will stop.
I run about in circles till I drop
Against a padlocked bulkhead in a yard
Where faces redden and the snow is hard.

IV

AT THE ALTAR

I sit at a gold table with my girl
Whose eyelids burn with brandy. What a whirl
Of Easter eggs is colored by the lights,
As the Norwegian dancer's crystaled tights
Flash with her naked leg's high-booted skate,
Like Northern Lights upon my watching plate.
The twinkling steel above me is a star;
I am a fallen Christmas tree. Our car
Races through seven red-lights—then the road
Is unpatrolled and empty, and a load
Of ply-wood with a tail-light makes us slow.
I turn and whisper in her ear. You know
I want to leave my mother and my wife,

You wouldn't have me tied to them for life . . .
Time runs, the windshield runs with stars. The past
Is cities from a train, until at last
Its escalating and black-windowed blocks
Recoil against a Gothic church. The clocks
Are tolling. I am dying. The shocked stones
Are falling like a ton of bricks and bones
That snap and splinter and descend in glass
Before a priest who mumbles through his Mass
And sprinkles holy water; and the Day
Breaks with its lightning on the man of clay,
Dies amara valde. Here the Lord
Is Lucifer in harness: hand on sword,
He watches me for Mother, and will turn
The bier and baby-carriage where I burn.

The Ghost

[AFTER SEXTUS PROPERTIUS]

A ghost is someone: death has left a hole
For the lead-colored soul to beat the fire:
    Cynthia leaves her dirty pyre
    And seems to coil herself and roll
        Under my canopy,
Love's stale and public playground, where I lie
And fill the run-down empire of my bed.
I see the street, her potter's field, is red
And lively with the ashes of the dead;

But she no longer sparkles off in smoke:
It is the body carted to the gate
    Last Friday, when the sizzling grate
    Left its charred furrows on her smock
        And ate into her hip.
A black nail dangles from a finger-tip
And Lethe oozes from her nether lip.
Her thumb-bones rattle on her brittle hands,
As Cynthia stamps and hisses and demands:

"Sextus has sleep already washed away
Your manhood? You forget the window-sill
    My sliding wore to slivers? Day
    Would break before the Seven Hills
        Saw Cynthia retreat
And climb your shoulders to the knotted sheet.
You shouldered me and galloped on bare feet
To lay me by the crossroads. Have no fear:
Notus, who snatched your promise, has no ear.

"But why did no one call in my deaf ear?
Your calling would have gained me one more day.
    Sextus, although you ran away
    You might have called and stopped my bier
        A second by your door.
No tears drenched a black toga for your whore
When broken tilestones bruised her face before
The Capitol. Would it have strained your purse
To scatter ten cheap roses on my hearse?

"The State will make Pompilia's Chloris burn:
I knew her secret when I kissed the skull
    Of Pluto in the tainted bowl.
    Let Nomas burn her books and turn
        Her poisons into gold;
The finger-prints upon the potsherd told
Her love. You let a slut, whose body sold
To Thracians, liquefy my golden bust
In the coarse flame that crinkled me to dust.

"If Chloris' bed has left you with your head,
Lover, I think you'll answer my arrears:
    My nurse is getting on in years,
    See that she gets a little bread—
        She never clutched your purse;
See that my little humpback hears no curse
From her close-fisted friend. But burn the verse
You bellowed half a lifetime in my name:
Why should you feed me to the fires of fame?

"I will not hound you, much as you have earned
It, Sextus: I shall reign in your four books—
    I swear this by the Hag who looks
    Into my heart where it was burned:
        Propertius, I kept faith;
If not, may serpents suck my ghost to death
And spit it with their forked and killing breath
Into the Styx where Agamemnon's wife
Founders in the green circles of her life.

"Beat the sycophant ivy from my urn,
That twists its binding shoots about my bones
    Where apple-sweetened Anio drones
    Through orchards that will never burn
        While honest Herakles,
My patron, watches. Anio, you will please
Me if you whisper upon sliding knees:
'Propertius, Cynthia is here:
She shakes her blossoms when my waters clear.'

"You cannot turn your back upon a dream,
For phantoms have their reasons when they come:
    We wander midnights: then the numb
    Ghost wades from the Lethean stream;
        Even the foolish dog
Stops its hell-raising mouths and casts its clog;
At cock-crow Charon checks us in his log.
Others can have you, Sextus; I alone
Hold: and I grind your manhood bone on bone."

In the Cage

The lifers file into the hall,
According to their houses—twos
Of laundered denim. On the wall
A colored fairy tinkles blues
And titters by the balustrade;
Canaries beat their bars and scream.
We come from tunnels where the spade
Pick-axe and hod for plaster steam
In mud and insulation. Here
The Bible-twisting Israelite
Fasts for his Harlem. It is night,
And it is vanity, and age
Blackens the heart of Adam. Fear,
The yellow chirper, beaks its cage.

At the Indian Killer's Grave

"Here, also, are the veterans of King Philip's War, who burned villages and slaughtered young and old, with pious fierceness, while the godly souls throughout the land were helping them with prayer."

HAWTHORNE

Behind King's Chapel what the earth has kept
Whole from the jerking noose of time extends
Its dark enigma to Jehoshaphat;
Or will King Philip plait
The just man's scalp in the wailing valley! Friends,
Blacker than these black stones the subway bends
About the dirty elm roots and the well
For the unchristened infants in the waste
Of the great garden rotten to its root;
Death, the engraver, puts forward his bone foot
And Grace-with-wings and Time-on-wings compel
All this antique abandon of the disgraced
To face Jehovah's buffets and his ends.

The dusty leaves and frizzled lilacs gear
This garden of the elders with baroque
And prodigal embellishments but smoke,
Settling upon the pilgrims and their grounds,
Espouses and confounds
Their dust with the off-scourings of the town;
The libertarian crown
Of England built their mausoleum. Here
A clutter of Bible and weeping willows guards
The stern Colonial magistrates and wards
Of Charles the Second, and the clouds

Weep on the just and unjust as they will—
For the poor dead cannot see Easter crowds
On Boston Common or the Beacon Hill
Where strangers hold the golden Statehouse dome
For good and always. Where they live is home:
A common with an iron railing: here
Frayed cables wreathe the spreading cenotaph
Of John and Mary Winslow and the laugh
Of Death is hacked in sandstone, in their year.

A green train grinds along its buried tracks
And screeches. When the great mutation racks
The Pilgrim Father's relics, will these plaques
Harness the spare-ribbed persons of the dead
To battle with the dragon? Philip's head
Grins on the platter, fouls in pantomime
The fingers of kept time:
"Surely, this people is but grass,"
He whispers, "this will pass;
But, Sirs, the trollop dances on your skulls
And breaks the hollow noddle like an egg
That thought the world an eggshell. Sirs, the gulls
Scream from the squelching wharf-piles, beg a leg
To crack their crops. The Judgment is at hand;
Only the dead are poorer in this world
Where State and elders thundered *raca*, hurled
Anathemas at nature and the land
That fed the hunter's gashed and green perfection—
Its settled mass concedes no outlets for your puns
And verbal Paradises. Your election,
Hawking above this slime
For souls as single as their skeletons,
Flutters and claws in the dead hand of time."

When you go down this man-hole to the drains,
The doorman barricades you in and out;
You wait upon his pleasure. All about
The pale, sand-colored, treeless chains
Of T-squared buildings strain
To curb the spreading of the braced terrain;
When you go down this hole, perhaps your pains
Will be rewarded well; no rough-cast house
Will bed and board you in King's Chapel. Here
A public servant putters with a knife
And paints the railing red
Forever, as a mouse
Cracks walnuts by the headstones of the dead
Whose chiseled angels peer
At you, as if their art were long as life.

I ponder on the railing at this park:
Who was the man who sowed the dragon's teeth,
That fabulous or fancied patriarch
Who sowed so ill for his descent, beneath
King's Chapel in this underworld and dark?
John, Matthew, Luke and Mark,
Gospel me to the Garden, let me come
Where Mary twists the warlock with her flowers—
Her soul a bridal chamber fresh with flowers
And her whole body an ecstatic womb,
As through the trellis peers the sudden Bridegroom.

Mr. Edwards and the Spider

I saw the spiders marching through the air,
Swimming from tree to tree that mildewed day
  In latter August when the hay
  Came creaking to the barn. But where
    The wind is westerly,
Where gnarled November makes the spiders fly
Into the apparitions of the sky,
They purpose nothing but their ease and die
Urgently beating east to sunrise and the sea;

What are we in the hands of the great God?
It was in vain you set up thorn and briar
  In battle array against the fire
  And treason crackling in your blood;
    For the wild thorns grow tame
And will do nothing to oppose the flame;
Your lacerations tell the losing game
You play against a sickness past your cure.
How will the hands be strong? How will the heart endure?

A very little thing, a little worm,
Or hourglass-blazoned spider, it is said,
  Can kill a tiger. Will the dead
  Hold up his mirror and affirm
    To the four winds the smell
And flash of his authority? It's well
If God who holds you to the pit of hell,
Much as one holds a spider, will destroy,
Baffle and dissipate your soul. As a small boy

On Windsor Marsh, I saw the spider die
When thrown into the bowels of fierce fire:
  There's no long struggle, no desire

To get up on its feet and fly—
      It stretches out its feet
    And dies. This is the sinner's last retreat;
    Yes, and no strength exerted on the heat
    Then sinews the abolished will, when sick
And full of burning, it will whistle on a brick.

      But who can plumb the sinking of that soul?
      Josiah Hawley, picture yourself cast
        Into a brick-kiln where the blast
        Fans your quick vitals to a coal—
          If measured by a glass,
    How long would it seem burning! Let there pass
    A minute, ten, ten trillion; but the blaze
    Is infinite, eternal: this is death,
To die and know it. This is the Black Widow, death.

After the Surprising Conversions

September twenty-second, Sir: today
I answer. In the latter part of May,
Hard on our Lord's Ascension, it began
To be more sensible. A gentleman
Of more than common understanding, strict
In morals, pious in behavior, kicked
Against our goad. A man of some renown,
An useful, honored person in the town,
He came of melancholy parents; prone
To secret spells, for years they kept alone—
His uncle, I believe, was killed of it:
Good people, but of too much or little wit.
I preached one Sabbath on a text from Kings;
He showed concernment for his soul. Some things
In his experience were hopeful. He
Would sit and watch the wind knocking a tree
And praise this countryside our Lord has made.
Once when a poor man's heifer died, he laid
A shilling on the doorsill; though a thirst
For loving shook him like a snake, he durst
Not entertain much hope of his estate
In heaven. Once we saw him sitting late
Behind his attic window by a light
That guttered on his Bible; through that night
He meditated terror, and he seemed
Beyond advice or reason, for he dreamed
That he was called to trumpet Judgment Day
To Concord. In the latter part of May
He cut his throat. And though the coroner
Judged him delirious, soon a noisome stir
Palsied our village. At Jehovah's nod
Satan seemed more let loose amongst us: God

Abandoned us to Satan, and he pressed
Us hard, until we thought we could not rest
Till we had done with life. Content was gone.
All the good work was quashed. We were undone.
The breath of God had carried out a planned
And sensible withdrawal from this land;
The multitude, once unconcerned with doubt,
Once neither callous, curious nor devout,
Jumped at broad noon, as though some peddler groaned
At it in its familiar twang: "My friend,
Cut your own throat. Cut your own throat. Now! Now!
September twenty-second, Sir, the bough
Cracks with the unpicked apples, and at dawn
The small-mouth bass breaks water, gorged with spawn

The Death of the Sheriff

"forsitan et Priami fuerint quae fata, requiras?"

NOLI ME TANGERE

We park and stare. A full sky of the stars
Wheels from the pumpkin setting of the moon
And sparks the windows of the yellow farm
Where the red-flanneled madmen look through bars
At windmills thrashing snowflakes by an arm
Of the Atlantic. Soon
The undertaker who collects antiques
Will let his motor idle at the door
And set his pine-box on the parlor floor.
Our homicidal sheriff howled for weeks;

We kiss. The State had reasons: on the whole,
It acted out of kindness when it locked
Its servant in this place and had him watched
Until an ordered darkness left his soul
A *tabula rasa;* when the Angel knocked
The sheriff laid his notched
Revolver on the table for the guest.
Night draws us closer in its bearskin wrap
And our loved sightless smother feels the tap
Of the blind stars descending to the west

To lay the Devil in the pit our hands
Are draining like a windmill. Who'll atone
For the unsearchable quicksilver heart
Where spiders stare their eyes out at their own
Spitting and knotted likeness? We must start:
Our aunt, his mother, stands
Singing *O Rock of Ages,* as the light

Wanderers show a man with a white cane
Who comes to take the coffin in his wain,
The thirsty Dipper on the arc of night.

Where the Rainbow Ends

I saw the sky descending, black and white,
Not blue, on Boston where the winters wore
The skulls to jack-o'-lanterns on the slates,
And Hunger's skin-and-bone retrievers tore
The chickadee and shrike. The thorn tree waits
Its victim and tonight
The worms will eat the deadwood to the foot
Of Ararat: the scythers, Time and Death,
Helmed locusts, move upon the tree of breath;
The wild ingrafted olive and the root

Are withered, and a winter drifts to where
The Pepperpot, ironic rainbow, spans
Charles River and its scales of scorched-earth miles.
I saw my city in the Scales, the pans
Of judgment rising and descending. Piles
Of dead leaves char the air—
And I am a red arrow on this graph
Of Revelations. Every dove is sold
The Chapel's sharp-shinned eagle shifts its hold
On serpent-Time, the rainbow's epitaph.

In Boston serpents whistle at the cold.
The victim climbs the altar steps and sings:
"Hosannah to the lion, lamb, and beast
Who fans the furnace-face of IS with wings:
I breathe the ether of my marriage feast."
At the high altar, gold
And a fair cloth. I kneel and the wings beat
My cheek. What can the dove of Jesus give
You now but wisdom, exile? Stand and live,
The dove has brought an olive branch to eat.

The Mills of
the Kavanaughs

The heron warps its neck, a broken pick,
To study its reflection on the scales,
Or knife-bright shards of water lilies, quick
In the dead autumn water with their snails
And water lice. Her ballet glasses hold
Him twisted by a fist of spruce, as dry
As flint and steel. She thinks: "The bird is old,
A cousin to all scholars; that is why
He will abet my thoughts of Kavanaugh,
Who gave the Mills its lumberyard and weir
In eighteen hundred, when our farmers saw
John Adams bring their Romish church a bell,
Cast—so the records claim—by Paul Revere.
The sticks of *Kavanaugh* are buried here—
Many of them, too many, Love, to tell—
Faithful to where their virgin forest fell."

And now the mussed blue-bottles bead her float:
Bringers of luck. Of luck? At worst, a rest
From counting blisters on her metal boat,
That spins and staggers. North and south and west:
A scene, perhaps, of Fragonard—her park,
Whose planted poplars scatter penny-leaves,
White underneath, like mussels to the dark
Chop of the shallows. Extirpation grieves
The sunken martyred laughter of the loon,
Where Harry's mother bathed in navy-blue
Stockings and skirts. But now, the afternoon
Is sullen, it is all that she can do
To lift the anchor. She can hardly row
Against these whitecaps—surely never lulled
For man and woman. Washing to and fro,
The floorboards bruise the lilies that she pulled.

"Even in August it was autumn—all
A pond could harbor." Now her matches fall
In dozens by her bobber to expire
As target-circles on the mirrored fire-
Escapes of *Kavanaugh*. She sees they hold
Her mirror to her—just a little cold;
A ground hog's looking glass. "The day is sharp
And short, Love, and its sun is like this carp,
Or goldfish, almost twenty inches long,
Panting, a weak old dog, below a prong
Of deadwood fallen from my copper beech;
The settling leaves embower its warmth. They reach
For my reflection, but it glides through shoal
Aground, to where the squirrel held its roots
And freehold, Love, unsliding, when our boots
Pattered—a life ago once—on its hole.

"I think we row together, for the stern
Jumps from my weaker stroke, and down the cove
Our house is floating, and the windows burn,
As if its underpinnings fed the stove.
Her window's open; look, she waits for us,
And types, until the clattering tin bell
Upon her room-large table tolls for us.
Listen, your mother's asking, *is it well?*
Yes, very well. He died outside the church
Like Harry Tudor. Now we near the sluice
And burial ground above the burlap mill;
I see you swing a string of yellow perch
About your head to fan off gnats that mill
And wail, as your disheartened shadow tries
The buried bedstead, where your body lies—
Time out of mind—a failing stand of spruce.

"God knows!" she marvels. "Harry, *Kavanaugh*
Was lightly given. Soon enough we saw
Death like the Bourbon after Waterloo,
Who learning and forgetting nothing, knew
Nothing but ruin. Why must we mistrust
Ourselves with Death who takes the world on trust?
Although God's brother, and himself a god,
Death whipped his horses through the startled sod;
For neither conscience nor omniscience warned
Him from his folly, when the virgin scorned
His courtship, and the quaking earth revealed
Death's desperation to the Thracian field.
And yet we think the virgin took no harm:
She gave herself because her blood was warm—
And for no other reason, Love, I gave
Whatever brought me gladness to the grave."

An old man in Concord forgets to go to morning service. He
falls asleep, while reading Vergil, and dreams that he is
Aeneas at the funeral of Pallas, an Italian prince.

The sun is blue and scarlet on my page,
And *yuck-a, yuck-a, yuck-a, yuck-a,* rage
The yellowhammers mating. Yellow fire
Blankets the captives dancing on their pyre,
And the scorched lictor screams and drops his rod.
Trojans are singing to their drunken God,
Ares. Their helmets catch on fire. Their files
Clank by the body of my comrade—miles
Of filings! Now the scythe-wheeled chariot rolls
Before their lances long as vaulting poles,
And I stand up and heil the thousand men,
Who carry Pallas to the bird-priest. Then
The bird-priest groans, and as his birds foretold,
I greet the body, lip to lip. I hold
The sword that Dido used. It tries to speak,
A bird with Dido's sworded breast. Its beak
Clangs and ejaculates the Punic word
I hear the bird-priest chirping like a bird.
I groan a little. "Who am I, and why?"
It asks, a boy's face, though its arrow-eye
Is working from its socket. "Brother, try,
O Child of Aphrodite, try to die:
To die is life." His harlots hang his bed
With feathers of his long-tailed birds. His head
Is yawning like a person. The plumes blow;
The beard and eyebrows ruffle. Face of snow,
You are the flower that country girls have caught,
A wild bee-pillaged honey-suckle brought
To the returning bridegroom—the design

Has not yet left it, and the petals shine;
The earth, its mother, has, at last, no help:
It is itself. The broken-winded yelp
Of my Phoenician hounds, that fills the brush
With snapping twigs and flying, cannot flush
The ghost of Pallas. But I take his pall,
Stiff with its gold and purple, and recall
How Dido hugged it to her, while she toiled,
Laughing—her golden threads, a serpent coiled
In cypress. Now I lay it like a sheet;
It clinks and settles down upon his feet,
The careless yellow hair that seemed to burn
Beforehand. Left foot, right foot—as they turn,
More pyres are rising: armored horses, bronze,
And gagged Italians, who must file by ones
Across the bitter river, when my thumb
Tightens into their wind-pipes. The beaks drum;
Their headman's cow-horned death's-head bites its tongue,
And stiffens, as it eyes the hero slung
Inside his feathered hammock on the crossed
Staves of the eagles that we winged. Our cost
Is nothing to the lovers, whoring Mars
And Venus, father's lover. Now his car's
Plumage is ready, and my marshals fetch
His squire, Acoctes, white with age, to hitch
Aethon, the hero's charger, and its ears
Prick, and it steps and steps, and stately tears
Lather its teeth; and then the harlots bring
The hero's charms and baton—but the King,
Vain-glorious Turnus, carried off the rest.
"I was myself, but Ares thought it best
The way it happened." At the end of time,
He sets his spear, as my descendants climb
The knees of Father Time, his beard of scalps,

His scythe, the arc of steel that crowns the Alps.
The elephants of Carthage hold those snows,
Turms of Numidian horse unsling their bows,
The flaming turkey-feathered arrows swarm
Beyond the Alps. "Pallas," I raise my arm
And shout, "Brother, eternal health. Farewell
Forever." Church is over, and its bell
Frightens the yellowhammers, as I wake
And watch the whitecaps wrinkle up the lake.
Mother's great-aunt, who died when I was eight,
Stands by our parlor sabre. "Boy, it's late.
Vergil must keep the Sabbath." Eighty years!
It all comes back. My Uncle Charles appears.
Blue-capped and bird-like. Phillips Brooks and Grant
Are frowning at his coffin, and my aunt,
Hearing his colored volunteers parade
Through Concord, laughs, and tells her English maid
To clip his yellow nostril hairs, and fold
His colors on him. . . . It is I. I hold
His sword to keep from falling, for the dust
On the stuffed birds is breathless, for the bust
Of young Augustus weighs on Vergil's shelf:
It scowls into my glasses at itself.

Her Dead Brother

The Lion of St. Mark's upon the glass
Shield in my window reddens, as the night
Enchants the swinging dories to its terrors,
And dulls your distant wind-stung eyes; alas,
Your portrait, coiled in German-silver hawsers, mirrors
The sunset as a dragon. Enough light
Remains to see you through your varnish. Giving
Your life has brought you closer to your friends;
Yes, it has brought you home. All's well that ends:
Achilles dead is greater than the living;

My mind holds you as I would have you live,
A wintering dragon. Summer was too short
When we went picnicking with telescopes
And crocking leather handbooks to that fort
Above the lank and heroned Sheepscot, where its slopes
Are clutched by hemlocks—spotting birds. I give
You back that idyll, brother. Was it more?
Remember riding, scotching with your spur
That four-foot milk-snake in a juniper?
Father shellacked it to the ice-house door.

Then you were grown; I left you on your own.
We will forget that August twenty-third,
When Mother motored with the maids to Stowe,
And the pale summer shades were drawn—so low
No one could see us; no, nor catch your hissing word,
As false as Cressid! Let our deaths atone:
The fingers on your sword-knot are alive,
And Hope, that fouls my brightness with its grace,
Will anchor in the narrows of your face.
My husband's Packard crunches up the drive.

Mother Marie Therese

[DROWNED IN 1912]

The speaker is a Canadian nun stationed in New Brunswick.

Old sisters at our Maris Stella House
Remember how the Mother's strangled grouse
And snow-shoe rabbits matched the royal glint
Of Pio Nono's vestments in the print
That used to face us, while our aching ring
Of stationary rockets saw her bring
Our cake. Often, when sunset hurt the rocks
Off Carthage, and surprised us knitting socks
For victims of the Franco-Prussian War,
Our scandal'd set her frowning at the floor;
And vespers struck like lightning through the gloom
And oaken ennui of her sitting room.
It strikes us now, but cannot re-inspire;
False, false and false, I mutter to my fire.
The good old times, ah yes! But good, that all's
Forgotten like our Province's cabals;
And Jesus, smiling earthward, finds it good;
For we were friends of Cato, not of God.
This sixtieth Christmas, I'm content to pray
For what life's shrinkage leaves from day to day;
And it's a sorrow to recall our young
Raptures for Mother, when her trophies hung,
Fresh in their blood and color, to convince
Even Probationers that Heaven's Prince,
Befriending, whispered: "Is it then so hard?
Tarry a little while, O disregard
Time's wings and armor, when it flutters down
Papal tiaras and the Bourbon crown;
For quickly, priest and prince will stand, their shields

Before each other's faces, in the fields,
Where, as I promised, virtue will compel
Michael and all his angels to repel
Satan's advances, till his forces lie
Beside the Lamb in blissful fealty."
Our Indian summer! Then, our skies could lift,
God willing; but an Indian brought the gift.
"A sword," said Father Turbot, "not a saint";
Yet He who made the Virgin without taint,
Chastised our Mother to the Rule's restraint.
Was it not fated that the sweat of Christ
Would wash the worldly serpent? Christ enticed
Her heart that fluttered, while she whipped her hounds
Into the quicksands of her manor grounds,
A lordly child, her habit fleur-de-lys'd—
There she dismounted, sick; with little heed,
Surrendered. Like Proserpina, who fell
Six months a year from earth to flower in hell;
She half-renounced by Candle, Book and Bell
Her flowers and fowling pieces for the Church.
She never spared the child and spoiled the birch;
And how she'd chide her novices, and pluck
Them by the ears for gabbling in Canuck,
While she was reading Rabelais from her chaise,
Or parroting the *Action Française*.
Her letter from the soi-disant French King,
And the less treasured golden wedding ring
Of her shy Bridegroom, yellow; and the regal
Damascus shot-guns, pegged upon her eagle
Emblems from Hohenzollern standards, rust.
Our world is passing; even she, whose trust
Was in its princes, fed the gluttonous gulls,
That whiten our Atlantic, when like skulls
They drift for sewage with the emerald tide.

Perpetual novenas cannot tide
Us past that drowning. After Mother died,
"An émigrée in this world and the next,"
Said Father Turbot, playing with his text.
Where is he? Surely, he is one of those,
Whom Christ and Satan spew! But no one knows
What's happened to that porpoise-bellied priest.
He lodged with us on Louis Neuvième's Feast,
And celebrated her memorial mass.
His bald spot tapestried by colored glass,
Our angels, Prussian blue and flaking red,
He squeaked and stuttered: "N-n-nothing is so d-dead
As a dead s-s-sister." Off Saint Denis' Head,
Our Mother, drowned on an excursion, sleeps.
Her billy goat, or its descendant, keeps
Watch on a headland, and I hear it bawl
Into this sixty-knot Atlantic squall,
"Mamamma's Baby," past Queen Mary's Neck,
The ledge at Carthage—almost to Quebec,
Where Monsieur de Montcalm, on Abraham's
Bosom, asleep, perceives our world that shams
His New World, lost—however it atones
For Wolfe, the Englishman, and Huron bones
And priests'. O Mother, here our snuffling crones
And cretins feared you, but I owe you flowers:
The dead, the sea's dead, has her sorrows, hours
On end to lie tossing to the east, cold,
Without bed-fellows, washed and bored and old,
Bilged by her thoughts, and worked on by the worms,
Until her fossil convent come to terms
With the Atlantic. Mother, there is room
Beyond our harbor. Past its wooden Boom
Now weak and waterlogged, that Frontenac
Once diagrammed, she welters on her back.
The bell-buoy, whom she called the Cardinal,

Dances upon her. If she hears at all,
She only hears it tolling to this shore,
Where our frost-bitten sisters know the roar
Of water, inching, always on the move
For virgins, when they wish the times were love,
And their hysterical hosannahs rouse
The loveless harems of the buck ruffed grouse,
Who drums, untroubled now, beside the sea—
As if he found our stern virginity
Contra naturam. We are ruinous;
God's Providence through time has mastered us:
Now all the bells are tongueless, now we freeze,
A later Advent, pruner of warped trees,
Whistles about our nunnery slabs, and yells,
And water oozes from us into wells;
A new year swells and stirs. Our narrow Bay
Freezes itself and us. We cannot say
Christ even sees us, when the ice floes toss
His statue, made by Hurons, on the cross,
That Father Turbot sank on Mother's mound—
A whirligig! Mother, we must give ground,
Little by little; but it does no good.
Tonight, while I am piling on more driftwood,
And stooping with the poker, you are here,
Telling your beads; and breathing in my ear,
You watch your orphan swording at her fears.
I feel you twitch my shoulder. No one hears
Us mock the sisters, as we used to, years
And years behind us, when we heard the spheres
Whirring *venite;* and we held our ears.
My mother's hollow sockets fill with tears.

The Fat Man in the Mirror

[AFTER WERFEL]

What's filling up the mirror? O, it is not I;
Hair-belly like a beaver's house? An old dog's eye?
    The forenoon was blue
    In the mad King's zoo
Nurse was swinging me so high, so high!

The bullies wrestled on the royal bowling green;
Hammers and sickles on their hoods of black sateen. . . .
    Sulking on my swing
    The tobacco King
Sliced apples with a pen-knife for the Queen.

This *I*, who used to mouse about the paraffined preserves,
And jammed a finger in the coffee-grinder, serves
    Time before the mirror.
    But this pursey terror . . .
Nurse, it is a person. *It is nerves.*

Where's the Queen-Mother waltzing like a top to staunch
The blood of Lewis, King of Faerie? Hip and haunch
    Lard the royal grotto;
    Straddling Lewis' motto,
Time, the Turk, its sickle on its paunch.

Nurse, Nurse, it rises on me . . . O, it starts to roll,
My apples, O, are ashes in the meerschaum bowl. . . .
    If you'd only come,
    If you'd only come,
Darling, if . . . The apples that I stole,

While Nurse and I were swinging in the Old One's eye . . .
Only a fat man with his beaver on his eye
    Only a fat man,
    Only a fat man
Bursts the mirror. O, it is not I!

Thanksgiving's Over

Thanksgiving night, 1942: a room on Third Avenue. Michael
dreams of his wife, a German-American Catholic, who leapt
from a window before she died in a sanatorium. The church
is the Franciscan church on 31st Street.

Thanksgiving night: Third Avenue was dead;
My fowl was soupbones. Fathoms overhead,
Snow warred on the El's world in the blank snow.
"Michael," she whispered, "just a year ago,
Even the shoreleave from the *Normandie*
Were weary of Thanksgiving; but they'd stop
And lift their hats. I watched their arctics drop
Below the birdstoup of the Anthony
And Child who guarded our sodality
For lay-Franciscans, Michael, till I heard
The birds inside me, and I knew the Third
Person possessed me, for I was the bird
Of Paradise, the parrot whose absurd
Garblings are glory. *Cherry ripe, ripe, ripe* . . ."

Winter had come on horseback, and the snow,
Hostile and unattended, wrapped my feet
In sheepskins. Where I'd stumbled from the street,
A red cement Saint Francis fed a row
Of toga'd boys with birds beneath a Child.
His candles flamed in tumblers, and He smiled.
"Romans!" she whispered, "look, these overblown
And bootless Brothers tell us we must go
Barefooted through the snow where birds recite:
Come unto us, our burden's light—light, light,
This burden that our marriage turned to stone!
O Michael, must we join the deaf and dumb

Breadline for children? Sit and listen," So
I sat. I counted to ten thousand, wound
My cowhorn beads from Dublin on my thumb,
And ground them. *Miserere?* Not a sound.

[FROM]

Life Studies

Beyond the Alps

(On the train from Rome to Paris. 1950, the year Pius XII
defined the dogma of Mary's bodily assumption.)

Reading how even the Swiss had thrown the sponge
in once again and Everest was still
unscaled, I watched our Paris Pullman lunge
mooning across the fallow Alpine snow.
O bella Roma! I saw our stewards go
forward on tiptoe banging on their gongs.
Life changed to landscape. Much against my will
I left the City of God where it belongs.
There the skirt-mad Mussolini unfurled
the eagle of Caesar. He was one of us
only, pure prose. I envy the conspicuous
waste of our grandparents on their grand tours—
long-haired Victorian sages bought the universe,
while breezing on their trust funds through the world.

When the Vatican made Mary's Assumption dogma,
the crowds at San Pietro screamed *Papá.*
The Holy Father dropped his shaving glass,
and listened. His electric razor purred,
his pet canary chirped on his left hand.
The lights of science couldn't hold a candle
to Mary risen—at one miraculous stroke,
angel-wing'd, gorgeous as a jungle bird!
But who believed this? Who could understand?
Pilgrims still kissed Saint Peter's brazen sandal.
The Duce's lynched, bare, booted skull still spoke.
God herded his people to the *coup de grâce—*
the costumed Switzers sloped their pikes to push,
O Pius, through the monstrous human crush. . . .

Our mountain-climbing train had come to earth.
Tired of the querulous hush-hush of the wheels,
the blear-eyed ego kicking in my berth
lay still, and saw Apollo plant his heels
on terra firma through the morning's thigh . . .
each backward, wasted Alp, a Parthenon,
fire-branded socket of the Cyclops' eye.
There were no tickets for that altitude
once held by Hellas, when the Goddess stood,
prince, pope, philosopher and golden bough,
pure mind and murder at the scything prow—
Minerva, the miscarriage of the brain.

Now Paris, our black classic, breaking up
like killer kings on an Etruscan cup.

Inauguration Day · January 1953

The snow had buried Stuyvesant.
The subways drummed the vaults. I heard
the El's green girders charge on Third,
Manhattan's truss of adamant,
that groaned in ermine, slummed on want. . . .
Cyclonic zero of the word,
God of our armies, who interred
Cold Harbor's blue immortals, Grant!
Horseman, your sword is in the groove!

Ice, ice. Our wheels no longer move.
Look, the fixed stars, all just alike
as lack-land atoms, split apart,
and the Republic summons Ike,
the mausoleum in her heart.

A Mad Negro Soldier Confined at Munich

"We're all Americans, except the Doc,
a Kraut DP, who kneels and bathes my eye.
The boys who floored me, two black maniacs, try
to pat my hands. Rounds, rounds! Why punch the clock?

In Munich the zoo's rubble fumes with cats;
hoydens with air-guns prowl the Koenigsplatz,
and pink the pigeons on the mustard spire.
Who but my girl-friend set the towns on fire?

Cathouses talk cold turkey to my guards;
I found my *Fräulein* stitching outing shirts
in the black forest of the colored wards—
lieutenants squawked like chickens in her skirts.

Her German language made my arteries harden—
I've no annuity from the pay we blew.
I chartered an aluminum canoe,
I had her six times in the English Garden.

Oh mama, mama, like a trolley-pole
sparking at contact, her electric shock—
the power-house! . . . The doctor calls our roll—
no knives, no forks. We file before the clock,

and fancy minnows, slaves of habit, shoot
like starlight through their air-conditioned bowl.
It's time for feeding. Each subnormal boot-
black heart is pulsing to its ant-egg dole."

Ford Madox Ford

1873–1939

The lobbed ball plops, then dribbles to the cup. . . .
(a birdie Fordie!) But it nearly killed
the ministers. Lloyd George was holding up
the flag. He gabbled, "Hop-toad, hop-toad, hop-toad!
Hueffer has used a niblick on the green;
it's filthy art, Sir, filthy art!"
You answered, "What is art to me and thee?
Will a blacksmith teach a midwife how to bear?"
That cut the puffing statesman down to size,
Ford. You said, "Otherwise,
I would have been general of a division." Ah Ford!
Was it war, the sport of kings, that your *Good Soldier*,
the best French novel in the language, taught
those Georgian Whig magnificoes at Oxford,
at Oxford decimated on the Somme?
Ford, five times black-balled for promotion,
then mustard-gassed voiceless some seven miles
behind the lines at Nancy or Belleau Wood:
you emerged in your "worn uniform,
gilt dragons on the revers of the tunic,"
a Jonah—O divorced, divorced
from the whale-fat of post-war London! Boomed,
cut, plucked and booted! In Provence, New York . . .
marrying, blowing . . . nearly dying
at Boulder, when the altitude
pressed the world on your heart,
and your audience, almost football-size,
shrank to a dozen, while you stood
mumbling, with fish-blue-eyes,
and mouth pushed out
fish-fashion, as if you gagged for air. . . .

Sandman! Your face, a childish O. The sun
is pernod-yellow and it gilds the heirs
of all the ages there on Washington
and Stuyvesant, your Lilliputian squares,
where writing turned your pockets inside out.
But master, mammoth mumbler, tell me why
the bales of your left-over novels buy
less than a bandage for your gouty foot.
Wheel-horse, O unforgetting elephant,
I hear you huffing at your old Brevoort,
Timon and Falstaff, while you heap the board
for publishers. Fiction! I'm selling short
your lies that made the great your equals. Ford,
you were a kind man and you died in want.

For George Santayana

1863–1952

In the heydays of 'forty-five,
bus-loads of souvenir-deranged
G.I.'s and officer-professors of philosophy
came crashing through your cell,
puzzled to find you still alive,
free-thinking Catholic infidel,
stray spirit, who'd found
the Church too good to be believed.
Later I used to dawdle
past Circus and Mithraic Temple
to *Santo Stefano* grown paper-thin
like you from waiting. . . .
There at the monastery hospital,
you wished those geese-girl sisters wouldn't bother
their heads and yours by praying for your soul:
"There is no God and Mary is His Mother."

Lying outside the consecrated ground
forever now, you smile
like Ser Brunetto running for the green
cloth at Verona—not like one
who loses, but like one who'd won . . .
as if your long pursuit of Socrates'
demon, man-slaying Alcibiades,
the demon of philosophy, at last had changed
those fleeting virgins into friendly laurel trees
at *Santo Stefano Rotondo*, when you died
near ninety,
still unbelieving, unconfessed and unreceived,
true to your boyish shyness of the Bride.
Old trooper, I see your child's red crayon pass,

bleeding deletions on the galleys you hold
under your throbbing magnifying glass,
that worn arena, where the whirling sand
and broken-hearted lions lick your hand
refined by bile as yellow as a lump of gold.

To Delmore Schwartz

(*Cambridge 1946*)

We couldn't even keep the furnace lit!
Even when we had disconnected it,
the antiquated
refrigerator gurgled mustard gas
through your mustard-yellow house,
and spoiled our long maneuvered visit
from T. S. Eliot's brother, Henry Ware. . . .

Your stuffed duck craned toward Harvard from my trunk:
its bill was a black whistle, and its brow
was high and thinner than a baby's thumb;
its webs were tough as toenails on its bough.
It was your first kill; you had rushed it home,
pickled in a tin wastebasket of rum—
it looked through us, as if it'd died dead drunk.
You must have propped its eyelids with a nail,
and yet it lived with us and met our stare,
Rabelaisian, lubricious, drugged. And there,
perched on my trunk and typing-table,
it cooled our universal
Angst a moment, Delmore. We drank and eyed
the chicken-hearted shadows of the world.
Underseas fellows, nobly mad,
we talked away our friends. "Let Joyce and Freud,
the Masters of Joy,
be our guests here," you said. The room was filled
with cigarette smoke circling the paranoid,
inert gaze of Coleridge, back
from Malta—his eyes lost in flesh, lips baked and black.
Your tiger kitten, *Oranges*,
cartwheeled for joy in a ball of snarls.

You said:
"*We poets in our youth begin in sadness;*
thereof in the end come despondency and madness;
Stalin has had two cerebral hemorrhages!"
The Charles
River was turning silver. In the ebb-
light of morning, we stuck
the duck
-'s web-
foot, like a candle, in a quart of gin we'd killed.

Words for Hart Crane

"When the Pulitzers showered on some dope
or screw who flushed our dry mouths out with soap,
few people would consider why I took
to stalking sailors, and scattered Uncle Sam's
phony gold-plated laurels to the birds.
Because I knew my Whitman like a book,
stranger in America, tell my country: I,
Catullus redivivus, once the rage
of the Village and Paris, used to play my role
of homosexual, wolfing the stray lambs
who hungered by the Place de la Concorde.
My profit was a pocket with a hole.
Who asks for me, the Shelley of my age,
must lay his heart out for my bed and board."

I

My Last Afternoon
with Uncle Devereux Winslow

1922: the stone porch of my Grandfather's summer house

I

"I won't go with you. I want to stay with Grandpa!"
That's how I threw cold water
on my Mother and Father's
watery martini pipe dreams at Sunday dinner.
. . . Fontainebleau, Mattapoisett, Puget Sound. . . .
Nowhere was anywhere after a summer
at my Grandfather's farm.
Diamond-pointed, athirst and Norman,
its alley of poplars
paraded from Grandmother's rose garden
to a scary stand of virgin pine,
scrub, and paths forever pioneering.

One afternoon in 1922,
I sat on the stone porch, looking through
screens as black-grained as drifting coal.
Tockytock, tockytock
clumped our Alpine, Edwardian cuckoo clock,
slung with strangled, wooden game.
Our farmer was cementing a root-house under the hill.
One of my hands was cool on a pile
of black earth, the other warm
on a pile of lime. All about me

were the works of my Grandfather's hands.
snapshots of his *Liberty Bell* silver mine;
his high school at *Stuttgart am Neckar;*
stogie-brown beams; fools'-gold nuggets;
octagonal red tiles,
sweaty with a secret dank, crummy with ant-stale;
a Rocky Mountain chaise longue,
its legs, shellacked saplings.
A pastel-pale Huckleberry Finn
fished with a broom straw in a basin
hollowed out of a millstone.
Like my Grandfather, the décor
was manly, comfortable,
overbearing, disproportioned.

What were those sunflowers? Pumpkins floating shoulder-high?
It was sunset, Sadie and Nellie
bearing pitchers of ice-tea,
oranges, lemons, mint, and peppermints,
and the jug of shandygaff,
which Grandpa made by blending half and half
yeasty, wheezing homemade sarsaparilla with beer.
The farm, entitled *Char-de-sa*
in the Social Register,
was named for my Grandfather's children:
Charlotte, Devereux, and Sarah.
No one had died there in my lifetime . . .
Only Cinder, our Scottie puppy
paralyzed from gobbling toads.
I sat mixing black earth and lime.

11

I was five and a half.
My formal pearl gray shorts
had been worn for three minutes.

My perfection was the Olympian
poise of my models in the imperishable autumn
display windows
of Rogers Peet's boys' store below the State House
in Boston. Distorting drops of water
pinpricked my face in the basin's mirror.
I was a stuffed toucan
with a bibulous, multicolored beak.

III

Up in the air
by the lakeview window in the billiards-room,
lurid in the doldrums of the sunset hour,
my Great Aunt Sarah
was learning *Samson and Delilah*.
She thundered on the keyboard of her dummy piano,
with gauze curtains like a boudoir table,
accordionlike yet soundless.
It had been bought to spare the nerves
of my Grandmother,
tone-deaf, quick as a cricket,
now needing a fourth for "Auction,"
and casting a thirsty eye
on Aunt Sarah, risen like the phoenix
from her bed of troublesome snacks and Tauchnitz classics.

Forty years earlier,
twenty, auburn headed,
grasshopper notes of genius!
Family gossip says Aunt Sarah
tilted her archaic Athenian nose
and jilted an Astor.
Each morning she practiced
on the grand piano at Symphony Hall,

deathlike in the off-season summer—
its naked Greek statues draped with purple
like the saints in Holy Week. . . .
On the recital day, she failed to appear.

I V

I picked with a clean finger nail at the blue anchor
on my sailor blouse washed white as a spinnaker.
What in the world was I wishing?
. . . A sail-colored horse browsing in the bullrushes . . .
A fluff of the west wind puffing
my blouse, kiting me over our seven chimneys,
troubling the waters. . . .
As small as sapphires were the ponds: *Quittacus, Snippituit,*
and *Assawompset,* halved by "the Island,"
where my Uncle's duck blind
floated in a barrage of smoke-clouds.
Double-barreled shotguns
stuck out like bundles of baby crow-bars.
A single sculler in a camouflaged kayak
was quacking to the decoys. . . .

At the cabin between the waters,
the nearest windows were already boarded.
Uncle Devereux was closing camp for the winter.
As if posed for "the engagement photograph,"
he was wearing his severe
war-uniform of a volunteer Canadian officer.
Daylight from the doorway riddled his student posters,
tacked helter-skelter on walls as raw as a boardwalk.
Mr. Punch, a water melon in hockey tights,
was tossing off a decanter of Scotch.
La Belle France in a red, white and blue toga
was accepting the arm of her "protector,"

the ingenu and porcine Edward VII.
The pre-war music hall belles
had goose necks, glorious signatures, beauty-moles,
and coils of hair like rooster tails.
The finest poster was two or three young men in khaki kilts
being bushwhacked on the veldt—
They were almost life-size. . . .

My Uncle was dying at twenty-nine.
"You are behaving like children,"
said my Grandfather,
when my Uncle and Aunt left their three baby daughters,
and sailed for Europe on a last honeymoon . . .
I cowered in terror.
I wasn't a child at all—
unseen and all-seeing, I was Agrippina
in the Golden House of Nero. . . .
Near me was the white measuring-door
my Grandfather had penciled with my Uncle's heights.
In 1911, he had stopped growing at just six feet.
While I sat on the tiles,
and dug at the anchor on my sailor blouse,
Uncle Devereux stood behind me.
He was as brushed as Bayard, our riding horse.
His face was putty.
His blue coat and white trousers
grew sharper and straighter.
His coat was a blue jay's tail,
his trousers were solid cream from the top of the bottle.
He was animated, hierarchical,
like a ginger snap man in a clothes-press.
He was dying of the incurable Hodgkin's disease. . . .
My hands were warm, then cool, on the piles
of earth and lime,

a black pile and a white pile. . . .
Come winter,
Uncle Devereux would blend to the one color.

Dunbarton

My Grandfather found
his grandchild's fogbound solitudes
sweeter than human society.

When Uncle Devereux died,
Daddy was still on sea-duty in the Pacific;
it seemed spontaneous and proper
for Mr. MacDonald, the farmer,
Karl, the chauffeur, and even my Grandmother
to say, "your Father." They meant my Grandfather.

He was my Father. I was his son.
On our yearly autumn get-aways from Boston
to the family graveyard in Dunbarton,
he took the wheel himself—
like an admiral at the helm.
Freed from Karl and chuckling over the gas he was saving,
he let his motor roller-coaster
out of control down each hill.
We stopped at the *Priscilla* in Nashua
for brownies and root-beer,
and later "pumped ship" together in the Indian Summer. . . .

At the graveyard, a suave Venetian Christ
gave a sheepdog's nursing patience
to Grandfather's Aunt Lottie,
his Mother, the stone but not the bones
of his Father, Francis.
Failing as when Francis Winslow could count
them on his fingers,
the clump of virgin pine still stretched patchy ostrich necks
over the disused millpond's fragrantly woodstained water,
a reddish blur,

like the ever-blackening wine-dark coat
in our portrait of Edward Winslow
once sheriff for George the Second,
the sire of bankrupt Tories.

Grandfather and I
raked leaves from our dead forebears,
defied the dank weather
with "dragon" bonfires.

Our helper, Mr. Burroughs,
had stood with Sherman at Shiloh—
his thermos of shockless coffee
was milk and grounds;
his illegal home-made claret
was as sugary as grape jelly
in a tumbler capped with paraffin.

I borrowed Grandfather's cane
carved with the names and altitudes
of Norwegian mountains he had scaled—
more a weapon than a crutch.
I lanced it in the fauve ooze for newts.
In a tobacco tin after capture, the umber yellow mature newts
lost their leopard spots,
lay grounded as numb
as scrolls of candied grapefruit peel.
I saw myself as a young newt,
neurasthenic, scarlet
and wild in the wild coffee-colored water.

In the mornings I cuddled like a paramour
in my Grandfather's bed,
while he scouted about the chattering greenwood stove.

Grandparents

They're altogether otherworldly now,
those adults champing for their ritual Friday spin
to pharmacist and five-and-ten in Brockton.
Back in my throw-away and shaggy span
of adolescence, Grandpa still waves his stick
like a policeman;
Grandmother, like a Mohammedan, still wears her thick
lavender mourning and touring veil;
the Pierce Arrow clears its throat in a horse stall.
Then the dry road dust rises to whiten
the fatigued elm leaves—
the nineteenth century, tired of children, is gone.
They're all gone into a world of light; the farm's my own.

The farm's my own!
Back there alone,
I keep indoors, and spoil another season.
I hear the rattly little country gramophone
racking its five foot horn:
"O Summer Time!"
Even at noon here the formidable
Ancien Régime still keeps nature at a distance. Five
green shaded light bulbs spider the billiards-table;
no field is greener than its cloth,
where Grandpa, dipping sugar for us both,
once spilled his demitasse.
His favorite ball, the number three,
still hides the coffee stain.
Never again
to walk there, chalk our cues,
insist on shooting for us both.
Grandpa! Have me, hold me, cherish me!
Tears smut my fingers. There
half my life-lease later,

I hold an *Illustrated London News*—;
disloyal still,
I doodle handlebar
mustaches on the last Russian Czar.

Commander Lowell

There were no undesirables or girls in my set,
when I was a boy at Mattapoisett—
only Mother, still her Father's daughter.
Her voice was still electric
with a hysterical, unmarried panic,
when she read to me from the Napoleon book.
Long-nosed Marie Louise
Hapsburg in the frontispiece
had a downright Boston bashfulness,
where she groveled to Bonaparte, who scratched his navel,
and bolted his food—just my seven years tall!
And I, bristling and manic,
skulked in the attic,
and got two hundred French generals by name,
from *A* to *V*—from Augereau to Vandamme.
I used to dope myself asleep,
naming those unpronounceables like sheep.

Having a naval officer
for my Father was nothing to shout
about to the summer colony at "Matt."
He wasn't at all "serious,"
when he showed up on the golf course,
wearing a blue serge jacket and numbly cut
white ducks he'd bought
at a Pearl Harbor commissariat . . .
and took four shots with his putter to sink his putt.
"Bob," they said, "golf's a game you really ought to know how
     to play,
if you play at all."
They wrote him off as "naval,"

naturally supposed his sport was sailing.
Poor Father, his training was engineering!
Cheerful and cowed
among the seadogs at the Sunday yacht club,
he was never one of the crowd.

"Anchors aweigh," Daddy boomed in his bathtub,
"Anchors aweigh,"
when Lever Brothers offered to pay
him double what the Navy paid.
I nagged for his dress sword with gold braid,
and cringed because Mother, new
caps on all her teeth, was born anew
at forty. With seamanlike celerity,
Father left the Navy,
and deeded Mother his property.

He was soon fired. Year after year,
he still hummed "Anchors aweigh" in the tub—
whenever he left a job,
he bought a smarter car.
Father's last employer
was Scudder, Stevens and Clark, Investment Advisors,
himself his only client.
While Mother dragged to bed alone,
read Menninger,
and grew more and more suspicious,
he grew defiant.
Night after night,
à la clarté déserte de sa lampe,
he slid his ivory Annapolis slide rule
across a pad of graphs—
piker speculations! In three years
he squandered sixty thousand dollars.

Smiling on all,
Father was once successful enough to be lost
in the mob of ruling-class Bostonians.
As early as 1928,
he owned a house converted to oil,
and redecorated by the architect
of St. Mark's School. . . . Its main effect
was a drawing room, "longitudinal as Versailles,"
its ceiling, roughened with oatmeal, was blue as the sea.
And once
nineteen, the youngest ensign in his class,
he was "the old man" of a gunboat on the Yangtze.

Terminal Days at Beverly Farms

At Beverly Farms, a portly, uncomfortable boulder
bulked in the garden's center—
an irregular Japanese touch.
After his Bourbon "old fashioned," Father,
bronzed, breezy, a shade too ruddy,
swayed as if on deck duty
under his six pointed star-lantern—
last July's birthday present.
He smiled his oval Lowell smile,
he wore his cream gabardine dinner-jacket,
and indigo cummerbund.
His head was efficient and hairless,
his newly dieted figure was vitally trim.

Father and Mother moved to Beverly Farms
to be a two-minute walk from the station,
half an hour by train from the Boston doctors.
They had no sea-view,
but sky-blue tracks of the commuters' railroad shone
like a double-barreled shotgun
through the scarlet late August sumac,
multiplying like cancer
at their garden's border.

Father had had two coronaries.
He still treasured underhand economies,
but his best friend was his little black Chevy,
garaged like a sacrificial steer
with gilded hooves,
yet sensationally sober,
and with less side than an old dancing pump.
The local dealer, a "buccaneer,"
had been bribed a "king's ransom"
to quickly deliver a car without chrome.

Each morning at eight-thirty,
inattentive and beaming,
loaded with his "calc" and "trig" books,
his clipper ship statistics,
and his ivory slide rule,
Father stole off with the Chevy
to loaf in the Maritime Museum at Salem.
He called the curator
"the commander of the Swiss Navy."

Father's death was abrupt and unprotesting.
His vision was still twenty-twenty.
After a morning of anxious, repetitive smiling,
his last words to Mother were:
"I feel awful."

Father's Bedroom

In my Father's bedroom:
blue threads as thin
as pen-writing on the bedspread,
blue dots on the curtains,
a blue kimono,
Chinese sandals with blue plush straps.
The broad-planked floor
had a sandpapered neatness.
The clear glass bed-lamp
with a white doily shade
was still raised a few
inches by resting on volume two
of Lafcadio Hearn's
Glimpses of Unfamiliar Japan.
Its warped olive cover
was punished like a rhinoceros hide.
In the flyleaf:
"Robbie from Mother."
Years later in the same hand:
"This book has had hard usage
on the Yangtze River, China.
It was left under an open
porthole in a storm."

For Sale

Poor sheepish plaything,
organized with prodigal animosity,
lived in just a year—
my Father's cottage at Beverly Farms
was on the market the month he died.
Empty, open, intimate,
its town-house furniture
had an on tiptoe air
of waiting for the mover
on the heels of the undertaker.
Ready, afraid
of living alone till eighty,
Mother mooned in a window,
as if she had stayed on a train
one stop past her destination.

Sailing Home from Rapallo

[*February 1954*]

Your nurse could only speak Italian,
but after twenty minutes I could imagine your final week,
and tears ran down my cheeks. . . .

When I embarked from Italy with my Mother's body,
the whole shoreline of the *Golfo di Genova*
was breaking into fiery flower.
The crazy yellow and azure sea-sleds
blasting like jack-hammers across
the *spumante*-bubbling wake of our liner,
recalled the clashing colors of my Ford.
Mother traveled first-class in the hold;
her *Risorgimento* black and gold casket
was like Napoleon's at the *Invalides*. . . .

While the passengers were tanning
on the Mediterranean in deck-chairs,
our family cemetery in Dunbarton
lay under the White Mountains
in the sub-zero weather.
The graveyard's soil was changing to stone—
so many of its deaths had been midwinter.
Dour and dark against the blinding snowdrifts,
its black brook and fir trunks were as smooth as masts.
A fence of iron spear-hafts
black-bordered its mostly Colonial grave-slates.
The only "unhistoric" soul to come here
was Father, now buried beneath his recent
unweathered pink-veined slice of marble.
Even the Latin of his Lowell motto:
Occasionem cognosce,

seemed too businesslike and pushing here,
where the burning cold illuminated
the hewn inscriptions of Mother's relatives:
twenty or thirty Winslows and Starks.
Frost had given their names a diamond edge. . . .

In the grandiloquent lettering on Mother's coffin,
Lowell had been misspelled *LOVEL*.
The corpse
was wrapped like *panettone* in Italian tinfoil.

During Fever

All night the crib creaks;
home from the healthy country to the sick city,
my daughter in fever
flounders in her chicken-colored sleeping bag.
"Sorry," she mumbles like her dim-bulb father, "sorry."

Mother, Mother!
as a gemlike undergraduate,
part criminal and yet a Phi Bete,
I used to barge home late.
Always by the banister
my milk-tooth mug of milk
was waiting for me on a plate
of Triskets.
Often with unadulterated joy,
Mother, we bent by the fire
rehashing Father's character—
when he thought we were asleep,
he'd tiptoed down the stairs
and chain the door.

Mother, your master-bedroom
looked away from the ocean.
You had a window-seat,
an electric blanket,
a silver hot-water bottle
monogrammed like a hip-flask,
Italian china fruity
with bunches and berries
and proper *putti*.
Gold, yellow and green,
the nuptial bed
was as big as a bathroom.

Born ten years and yet an aeon
too early for the twenties,
Mother, you smile
as if you saw your Father
inches away yet hidden, as when he groused behind a screen
over a National Geographic Magazine,
whenever young men came to court you
back in those settled years of World War One.
Terrible that old life of decency
without unseemly intimacy
or quarrels, when the unemancipated woman
still had her Freudian papá and maids!

Waking in the Blue

The night attendant, a B.U. sophomore,
rouses from the mare's-nest of his drowsy head
propped on *The Meaning of Meaning*.
He catwalks down our corridor.
Azure day
makes my agonized blue window bleaker.
Crows maunder on the petrified fairway.
Absence! My heart grows tense
as though a harpoon were sparring for the kill.
(This is the house for the "mentally ill.")

What use is my sense of humor?
I grin at Stanley, now sunk in his sixties,
once a Harvard all-American fullback
(if such were possible!),
still hoarding the build of a boy in his twenties,
as he soaks, a ramrod
with the muscle of a seal
in his long tub,
vaguely urinous from the Victorian plumbing.
A kingly granite profile in a crimson golf cap,
worn all day, all night,
he thinks only of his figure,
of slimming on sherbet and ginger ale—
more cut off from words than a seal.

This is the way day breaks in Bowditch Hall at McLean's;
the hooded night lights bring out "Bobbie,"
Porcellian '29,
a replica of Louis XVI
without the wig—
redolent and roly-poly as a sperm whale,
as he swashbuckles about in his birthday suit
and horses at chairs.

These victorious figures of bravado ossified young.

In between the limits of day,
hours and hours go by under the crew haircuts
and slightly too little nonsensical bachelor twinkle
of the Roman Catholic attendants.
(There are no Mayflower
screwballs in the Catholic Church.)

After a hearty New England breakfast,
I weigh two hundred pounds
this morning. Cock of the walk,
I strut in my turtle-necked French sailor's jersey
before the metal shaving mirrors,
and see the shaky future grow familiar
in the pinched, indigenous faces
of these thoroughbred mental cases,
twice my age and half my weight.
We are all old-timers,
each of us holds a locked razor.

Home After Three Months Away

Gone now the baby's nurse,
a lioness who ruled the roost
and made the Mother cry.
She used to tie
gobbets of porkrind in bowknots of gauze—
three months they hung like soggy toast
on our eight foot magnolia tree,
and helped the English sparrows
weather a Boston winter.

Three months, three months!
Is Richard now himself again?
Dimpled with exaltation,
my daughter holds her levee in the tub.
Our noses rub,
each of us pats a stringy lock of hair—
they tell me nothing's gone.
Though I am forty-one,
not forty now, the time I put away
was child's-play. After thirteen weeks
my child still dabs her cheeks
to start me shaving. When
we dress her in her sky-blue corduroy,
she changes to a boy,
and floats my shaving brush
and washcloth in the flush. . . .
Dearest, I cannot loiter here
in lather like a polar bear.

Recuperating, I neither spin nor toil.
Three stories down below,
a choreman tends our coffin's length of soil,
and seven horizontal tulips blow.

Just twelve months ago,
these flowers were pedigreed
imported Dutchmen; now no one need
distinguish them from weed.
Bushed by the late spring snow,
they cannot meet
another year's snowballing enervation.

I keep no rank nor station.
Cured, I am frizzled, stale and small.

Memories of West Street and Lepke

Only teaching on Tuesdays, book-worming
in pajamas fresh from the washer each morning,
I hog a whole house on Boston's
"hardly passionate Marlborough Street,"
where even the man
scavenging filth in the back alley trash cans,
has two children, a beach wagon, a helpmate,
and is a "young Republican."
I have a nine months' daughter,
young enough to be my granddaughter.
Like the sun she rises in her flame-flamingo infants' wear.

These are the tranquillized *Fifties*,
and I am forty. Ought I to regret my seedtime?
I was a fire-breathing Catholic C.O.,
and made my manic statement,
telling off the state and president, and then
sat waiting sentence in the bull pen
beside a Negro boy with curlicues
of marijuana in his hair.

Given a year,
I walked on the roof of the West Street Jail, a short
enclosure like my school soccer court,
and saw the Hudson River once a day
through sooty clothesline entanglements
and bleaching khaki tenements.
Strolling, I yammered metaphysics with Abramowitz,
a jaundice-yellow ("it's really tan")
and fly-weight pacifist,
so vegetarian,

he wore rope shoes and preferred fallen fruit.
He tried to convert Bioff and Brown,
the Hollywood pimps, to his diet.
Hairy, muscular, suburban,
wearing chocolate double-breasted suits,
they blew their tops and beat him black and blue.

I was so out of things, I'd never heard
of the Jehovah's Witnesses.
"Are you a C.O.?" I asked a fellow jailbird.
"No," he answered, "I'm a J.W."
He taught me the "hospital tuck,"
and pointed out the T-shirted back
of *Murder Incorporated's* Czar Lepke,
there piling towels on a rack,
or dawdling off to his little segregated cell full
of things forbidden the common man:
a portable radio, a dresser, two toy American
flags tied together with a ribbon of Easter palm.
Flabby, bald, lobotomized,
he drifted in a sheepish calm,
where no agonizing reappraisal
jarred his concentration on the electric chair—
hanging like an oasis in his air
of lost connections. . . .

Man and Wife

Tamed by *Miltown*, we lie on Mother's bed;
the rising sun in war paint dyes us red;
in broad daylight her gilded bed-posts shine,
abandoned, almost Dionysian.
At last the trees are green on Marlborough Street,
blossoms on our magnolia ignite
the morning with their murderous five days' white.
All night I've held your hand,
as if you had
a fourth time faced the kingdom of the mad—
its hackneyed speech, its homicidal eye—
and dragged me home alive. . . . Oh my *Petite*,
clearest of all God's creatures, still all air and nerve:
you were in your twenties, and I,
once hand on glass
and heart in mouth,
outdrank the Rahvs in the heat
of Greenwich Village, fainting at your feet—
too boiled and shy
and poker-faced to make a pass,
while the shrill verve
of your invective scorched the traditional South.

Now twelve years later, you turn your back.
Sleepless, you hold
your pillow to your hollows like a child;
your old-fashioned tirade—
loving, rapid, merciless—
breaks like the Atlantic Ocean on my head.

"To Speak of Woe That Is in Marriage"

"It is the future generation that presses into being by means of these exuberant feelings and supersensible soap bubbles of ours."

SCHOPENHAUER

"The hot night makes us keep our bedroom windows open.
Our magnolia blossoms. Life begins to happen.
My hopped up husband drops his home disputes,
and hits the streets to cruise for prostitutes,
free-lancing out along the razor's edge.
This screwball might kill his wife, then take the pledge.
Oh the monotonous meanness of his lust. . . .
It's the injustice . . . he is so unjust—
whiskey-blind, swaggering home at five.
My only thought is how to keep alive.
What makes him tick? Each night now I tie
ten dollars and his car key to my thigh. . . .
Gored by the climacteric of his want,
he stalls above me like an elephant."

Skunk Hour

[FOR ELIZABETH BISHOP]

Nautilus Island's hermit
heiress still lives through winter in her Spartan cottage;
her sheep still graze above the sea.
Her son's a bishop. Her farmer
is first selectman in our village;
she's in her dotage.

Thirsting for
the hierarchic privacy
of Queen Victoria's century,
she buys up all
the eyesores facing her shore,
and lets them fall.

The season's ill—
we've lost our summer millionaire,
who seemed to leap from an L. L. Bean
catalogue. His nine-knot yawl
was auctioned off to lobstermen.
A red fox stain covers Blue Hill.

And now our fairy
decorator brightens his shop for fall;
his fishnet's filled with orange cork,
orange, his cobbler's bench and awl;
there is no money in his work,
he'd rather marry.

One dark night,
my Tudor Ford climbed the hill's skull;

I watched for love-cars. Lights turned down,
they lay together, hull to hull,
where the graveyard shelves on the town. . . .
My mind's not right.

A car radio bleats,
"Love, O careless Love. . . ." I hear
my ill-spirit sob in each blood cell,
as if my hand were at its throat. . . .
I myself am hell;
nobody's here—

only skunks, that search
in the moonlight for a bite to eat.
They march on their soles up Main Street:
white stripes, moonstruck eyes' red fire
under the chalk-dry and spar spire
of the Trinitarian Church.

I stand on top
of our back steps and breathe the rich air—
a mother skunk with her column of kittens swills the garbage
        pail.
She jabs her wedge-head in a cup
of sour cream, drops her ostrich tail,
and will not scare.

For the Union Dead

Water

It was a Maine lobster town—
each morning boatloads of hands
pushed off for granite
quarries on the islands,

and left dozens of bleak
white frame houses stuck
like oyster shells
on a hill of rock,

and below us, the sea lapped
the raw little match-stick
mazes of a weir,
where the fish for bait were trapped.

Remember? We sat on a slab of rock.
From this distance in time,
it seems the color
of iris, rotting and turning purpler,

but it was only
the usual gray rock
turning the usual green
when drenched by the sea.

The sea drenched the rock
at our feet all day,
and kept tearing away
flake after flake.

One night you dreamed
you were a mermaid clinging to a wharf-pile,
and trying to pull
off the barnacles with your hands.

We wished our two souls
might return like gulls
to the rock. In the end,
the water was too cold for us.

The Old Flame

My old flame, my wife!
Remember our lists of birds?
One morning last summer, I drove
by our house in Maine. It was still
on top of its hill—

Now a red ear of Indian maize
was splashed on the door.
Old Glory with thirteen stars
hung on a pole. The clapboard
was old-red schoolhouse red.

Inside, a new landlord,
a new wife, a new broom!
Atlantic seaboard antique shop
pewter and plunder
shone in each room.

A new frontier!
No running next door
now to phone the sheriff
for his taxi to Bath
and the State Liquor Store!

No one saw your ghostly
imaginary lover
stare through the window,
and tighten
the scarf at his throat.

Health to the new people,
health to their flag, to their old
restored house on the hill!
Everything had been swept bare,
furnished, garnished, and aired.

Everything's changed for the best—
how quivering and fierce we were,
there snowbound together,
simmering like wasps
in our tent of books!

Poor ghost, old love, speak
with your old voice
of flaming insight
that kept us awake all night.
In one bed and apart,

we heard the plow
groaning up hill—
a red light, then a blue,
as it tossed off the snow
to the side of the road.

Middle Age

Now the midwinter grind
is on me, New York
drills through my nerves,
as I walk
the chewed-up streets.

At forty-five,
what next, what next?
At every corner,
I meet my Father,
my age, still alive.

Father, forgive me
my injuries,
as I forgive
those I
have injured!

You never climbed
Mount Sion, yet left
dinosaur
death-steps on the crust,
where I must walk.

The Mouth of the Hudson

[FOR ESTHER BROOKS]

A single man stands like a bird-watcher,
and scuffles the pepper and salt snow
from a discarded, gray
Westinghouse Electric cable drum.
He cannot discover America by counting
the chains of condemned freight-trains
from thirty states. They jolt and jar
and junk in the siding below him.
He has trouble with his balance.
His eyes drop,
and he drifts with the wild ice
ticking seaward down the Hudson,
like the blank sides of a jig-saw puzzle.

The ice ticks seaward like a clock.
A Negro toasts
wheat-seeds over the coke-fumes
of a punctured barrel.
Chemical air
sweeps in from New Jersey,
and smells of coffee.

Across the river,
ledges of suburban factories tan
in the sulphur-yellow sun
of the unforgivable landscape.

Fall 1961

Back and forth, back and forth
goes the tock, tock, tock
of the orange, bland, ambassadorial
face of the moon
on the grandfather clock.

All autumn, the chafe and jar
of nuclear war;
we have talked our extinction to death.
I swim like a minnow
behind my studio window.

Our end drifts nearer,
the moon lifts,
radiant with terror.
The state
is a diver under a glass bell.

A father's no shield
for his child.
We are like a lot of wild
spiders crying together,
but without tears.

Nature holds up a mirror.
One swallow makes a summer.
It's easy to tick
off the minutes,
but the clockhands stick.

Back and forth!
Back and forth, back and forth—
my one point of rest
is the orange and black
oriole's swinging nest!

Florence

[FOR MARY MCCARTHY]

I long for the black ink,
cuttlefish, April, Communists
and brothels of Florence—
everything, even the British
fairies who haunted the hills,
even the chills and fever
that came once a month
and forced me to think.
The apple was more human there than here,
but it took a long time for the blinding
golden rind to mellow.

How vulnerable the horseshoe crabs
dredging the bottom like flat-irons
in their antique armor,
with their swordgrass blackbone tails,
made for a child to grab
and throw strangling ashore!

Oh Florence, Florence, patroness
of the lovely tyrannicides!
Where the tower of the Old Palace
pierces the sky
like a hypodermic needle,
Perseus, David and Judith,
lords and ladies of the Blood,
Greek demi-gods of the Cross,
rise sword in hand
above the unshaven,
formless decapitation
of the monsters, tubs of guts,
mortifying chunks for the pack.

Pity the monsters!
Pity the monsters!
Perhaps, one always took the wrong side—
Ah, to have known, to have loved
too many Davids and Judiths!
My heart bleeds black blood for the monster.
I have seen the Gorgon.
The erotic terror
of her helpless, big bosomed body
lay like slop.
Wall-eyed, staring the despot to stone,
her severed head swung
like a lantern in the victor's hand.

Eye and Tooth

My whole eye was sunset red,
the old cut cornea throbbed,
I saw things darkly,
as through an unwashed goldfish globe.

I lay all day on my bed.
I chain-smoked through the night,
learning to flinch
at the flash of the matchlight.

Outside, the summer rain,
a simmer of rot and renewal,
fell in pinpricks.
Even new life is fuel.

My eyes throb.
Nothing can dislodge
the house with my first tooth
noosed in a knot to the doorknob.

Nothing can dislodge
the triangular blotch
of rot on the red roof,
a cedar hedge, or the shade of a hedge.

No ease from the eye
of the sharp-shinned hawk in the birdbook there,
with reddish-brown buffalo hair
on its shanks, one ascetic talon

clasping the abstract imperial sky.
It says:
an eye for an eye,
a tooth for a tooth.

No ease for the boy at the keyhole,
his telescope,
when the women's white bodies flashed
in the bathroom. Young, my eyes began to fail.

Nothing! No oil
for the eye, nothing to pour
on those waters or flames.
I am tired. Everyone's tired of my turmoil.

Alfred Corning Clark

[*1916–1961*]

You read the *New York Times*
every day at recess,
but in its dry
obituary, a list
of your wives, nothing is news,
except the ninety-five
thousand dollar engagement ring
you gave the sixth.
Poor rich boy,
you were unreasonably adult
at taking your time,
and died at forty-five.
Poor Al Clark,
behind your enlarged,
hardly recognizable photograph,
I feel the pain.
You were alive. You are dead.
You wore bow-ties and dark
blue coats, and sucked
wintergreen or cinnamon lifesavers
to sweeten your breath.
There must be something—
some one to praise
your triumphant diffidence,
your refusal of exertion,
the intelligence
that pulsed in the sensitive,
pale concavities of your forehead.
You never worked,
and were third in the form.
I owe you something—

I was befogged,
and you were too bored,
quick and cool to laugh.
You are dear to me, Alfred;
our reluctant souls united
in our unconventional
illegal games of chess
on the St. Mark's quadrangle.
You usually won—
motionless
as a lizard in the sun.

Child's Song

My cheap toy lamp
gives little light
all night, all night,
when my muscles cramp.

Sometimes I touch your hand
across my cot,
and our fingers knot,
but there's no hand

to take me home—
no Caribbean
island, where even
the shark is at home.

It must be heaven.
There on that island
the white sand shines
like a birchwood fire.

Help, saw me in two,
put me on the shelf!
Sometimes the little muddler
can't stand itself!

The Public Garden

Burnished, burned-out, still burning as the year
you lead me to our stamping ground.
The city and its cruising cars surround
the Public Garden. All's alive—
the children crowding home from school at five,
punting a football in the bricky air,
the sailors and their pick-ups under trees
with Latin labels. And the jaded flock
of swanboats paddles to its dock.
The park is drying.
Dead leaves thicken to a ball
inside the basin of a fountain, where
the heads of four stone lions stare
and suck on empty fawcets. Night
deepens. From the arched bridge, we see
the shedding park-bound mallards, how they keep
circling and diving in the lanternlight,
searching for something hidden in the muck.
And now the moon, earth's friend, that cared so much
for us, and cared so little, comes again—
always a stranger! As we walk,
it lies like chalk
over the waters. Everything's aground.
Remember summer? Bubbles filled
the fountain, and we splashed. We drowned
in Eden, while Jehovah's grass-green lyre
was rustling all about us in the leaves
that gurgled by us, turning upside down . . .
The fountain's failing waters flash around
the garden. Nothing catches fire.

Myopia: a Night

Bed, glasses off, and all's
ramshackle, streaky, weird
for the near-sighted, just
a foot away.
                    The light's
still on an instant. Here
are the blurred titles, here
the books are blue hills, browns,
greens, fields, or color.
                            This
is the departure strip,
the dream-road. Whoever built it
left numbers, words and arrows.
He had to leave in a hurry.

I see
a dull and alien room,
my cell of learning,
white, brightened by white pipes,
ramrods of steam . . . I hear
the lonely metal breathe
and gurgle like the sick.
And yet my eyes avoid
that room. No need to see.
No need to know I hoped
its blank, foregoing whiteness
would burn away the blur,
as my five senses clenched
their teeth, thought stitched to thought,
as through a needle's eye . . .

I see the morning star . . .

Think of him in the Garden,
that seed of wisdom, Eve's
seducer, stuffed with man's
corruption, stuffed with triumph:
Satan triumphant in
the Garden! In a moment,
all that blinding brightness
changed into a serpent,
lay grovelling on its gut.

What has disturbed this household?
Only a foot away,
the familiar faces blur.
At fifty we're so fragile,
a feather . . .

The things of the eye are done.
On the illuminated black dial,
green ciphers of a new moon—
one, two, three, four, five, six!
I breathe and cannot sleep.
Then morning comes,
saying, "This was a night."

The Drinker

The man is killing time—there's nothing else.
No help now from the fifth of Bourbon
chucked helter-skelter into the river,
even its cork sucked under.

Stubbed before-breakfast cigarettes
burn bull's-eyes on the bedside table;
a plastic tumbler of alka seltzer
champagnes in the bathroom.

No help from his body, the whale's
warm-hearted blubber, foundering down
leagues of ocean, gasping whiteness.
The barbed hooks fester. The lines snap tight.

When he looks for neighbors, their names blur in the window,
his distracted eye sees only glass sky.
His despair has the galvanized color
of the mop and water in the galvanized bucket.

Once she was close to him
as water to the dead metal.

He looks at her engagements inked on her calendar.
A list of indictments.
At the numbers in her thumbed black telephone book.
A quiver full of arrows.

Her absence hisses like steam,
the pipes sing . . .
even corroded metal somehow functions.
He snores in his iron lung,

and hears the voice of Eve,
beseeching freedom from the Garden's
perfect and ponderous bubble. No voice
outsings the serpent's flawed, euphoric hiss.

The cheese wilts in the rat-trap,
the milk turns to junket in the cornflakes bowl,
car keys and razor blades
shine in an ashtray.

Is he killing time? Out on the street,
two cops on horseback clop through the April rain
to check the parking meter violations—
their oilskins yellow as forsythia.

Follow its lazy main street lounging
from the alms house to Gallows Hill
along a flat, unvaried surface
covered with wooden houses
aged by yellow drain
like the unhealthy hair of an old dog.
You'll walk to no purpose
in Hawthorne's Salem.

I cannot resilver the smudged plate.

I drop to Hawthorne, the customs officer,
measuring coal and mostly trying to keep warm—
to the stunted black schooner,
the dismal South-end dock,
the wharf-piles with their fungus of ice.
On State Street
a steeple with a glowing dial-clock
measures the weary hours,
the merciless march of professional feet.

Even this shy distrustful ego
sometimes walked on top of the blazing roof,
and felt those flashes
that char the discharged cells of the brain.

Look at the faces—
Longfellow, Lowell, Holmes and Whittier!
Study the grizzled silver of their beards.
Hawthorne's picture,
however, has a blond mustache
and golden General Custer scalp.
He looks like a Civil War officer.
He shines in the firelight. His hard
survivor's smile is touched with fire.

Leave him alone for a moment or two,
and you'll see him with his head
bent down, brooding, brooding,
eyes fixed on some chip,
some stone, some common plant,
the commonest thing,
as if it were the clue.
The disturbed eyes rise,
furtive, foiled, dissatisfied
from meditation on the true
and insignificant.

Jonathan Edwards in Western Massachusetts

Edwards' great millstone and rock
of hope has crumbled, but the square
white houses of his flock
stand in the open air,

out in the cold,
like sheep outside the fold.
Hope lives in doubt.
Faith is trying to do without

faith. In western Massachusetts,
I could almost feel the frontier
crack and disappear.
Edwards thought the world would end there.

We know how the world will end,
but where is paradise, each day further
from the Pilgrim's blues for England
and the Promised Land.

Was it some country house
that seemed as if it were
Whitehall, if the Lord were there?
so nobly did he live.

Gardens designed
that the breath of flowers in the wind,
or crushed underfoot,
came and went like warbling music?

Bacon's great oak grove
he refused to sell,
when he fell,
saying, "Why should I sell my feathers?"

Ah paradise! Edwards,
I would be afraid
to meet you there as a shade.
We move in different circles.

As a boy, you built a booth
in a swamp for prayer;
lying on your back,
you saw the spiders fly,

basking at their ease,
swimming from tree to tree—
so high, they seemed tacked to the sky.
You knew they would die.

Poor country Berkeley at Yale,
you saw the world was soul,
the soul of God! The soul
of Sarah Pierrepont!

So filled with delight in the Great Being,
she hardly cared for anything—
walking the fields, sweetly singing,
conversing with some one invisible.

Then God's love shone in sun, moon and stars,
on earth, in the waters,
in the air, in the loose winds,
which used to greatly fix your mind.

Often she saw you come home from a ride
or a walk, your coat dotted with thoughts
you had pinned there
on slips of paper.

You gave
her Pompey, a Negro slave,
and eleven children.
Yet people were spiders

in your moment of glory,
at the Great Awakening—"Alas, how many
in this very meeting house are more than likely
to remember my discourse in hell!"

The meeting house remembered!
You stood on stilts in the air,
but you fell from your parish.
"All rising is by a winding stair."

On my pilgrimage to Northampton,
I found no relic,
except the round slice of an oak
you are said to have planted.

It was flesh-colored, new,
and a common piece of kindling,
only fit for burning.
You too must have been green once.

White wig and black coat,
all cut from one cloth,
and designed
like your mind!

I love you faded,
old, exiled and afraid
to leave your last flock, a dozen
Housatonic Indian children;

afraid to leave
all your writing, writing, writing,
denying the Freedom of the Will.
You were afraid to be president

of Princeton, and wrote:
"My deffects are well known;
I have a constitution
peculiarly unhappy:

flaccid solids,
vapid, sizzy, scarse fluids,
causing a childish weakness,
a low tide of spirits.

I am contemptible,
stiff and dull.

Why should I leave behind
my delight and entertainment,
those studies
that have swallowed up my mind?"

Tenth Muse, Oh my heart-felt Sloth,
how often now you come to my bed,
thin as a canvas in your white and red
check dresses like a table cloth,
my Dearest, settling like my shroud!

Yes, yes, I ought to remember Moses
jogging down on his mule from the Mount
with the old law, the old mistake,
safe in his saddlebags, and chiseled
on the stones we cannot bear or break.

Here waiting, here waiting for an answer
from this malignant surf of unopened letters,
always reaching land too late,
as fact and abstraction accumulate,
and the signature fades from the paper—

I like to imagine it must have been simpler
in the days of Lot,
or when Greek and Roman picturebook
gods sat combing their golden beards,
each on his private hill or mountain.

But I suppose even God was born
too late to trust the old religion—
all those settings out
that never left the ground,
beginning in wisdom, dying in doubt.

The Neo-Classical Urn

I rub my head and find a turtle shell
stuck on a pole,
each hair electrical
with charges, and the juice alive
with ferment. Bubbles drive
the motor, always purposeful . . .
Poor head!
How its skinny shell once hummed,
as I sprinted down the colonnade
of bleaching pines, cylindrical
clipped trunks without a twig between them. Rest!
I could not rest. At full run on the curve,
I left the cast stone statue of a nymph,
her soaring armpits and her one bare breast,
gray from the rain and graying in the shade,
as on, on, in sun, the pathway now a dyke,
I swerved between two water bogs,
two seines of moss, and stooped to snatch
the painted turtles on dead logs.
In that season of joy,
my turtle catch
was thirty-three,
dropped splashing in our garden urn,
like money in the bank,
the plop and splash
of turtle on turtle,
fed raw gobs of hash . . .

Oh neo-classical white urn, Oh nymph,
Oh lute! The boy was pitiless who strummed
their elegy,
for as the month wore on,
the turtles rose,
and popped up dead on the stale scummed

surface—limp wrinkled heads and legs withdrawn
in pain. What pain? A turtle's nothing. No
grace, no cerebration, less free will
than the mosquito I must kill—
nothings! Turtles! I rub my skull,
that turtle shell,
and breathe their dying smell,
still watch their crippled last survivors pass,
and hobble humpbacked through the grizzled grass.

July in Washington

The stiff spokes of this wheel
touch the sore spots of the earth.

On the Potomac, swan-white
power launches keep breasting the sulphurous wave.

Otters slide and dive and slick back their hair,
raccoons clean their meat in the creek.

On the circles, green statues ride like South American
liberators above the breeding vegetation—

prongs and spearheads of some equatorial
backland that will inherit the globe.

The elect, the elected . . . they come here bright as dimes,
and die disheveled and soft.

We cannot name their names, or number their dates—
circle on circle, like rings on a tree—

but we wish the river had another shore,
some farther range of delectable mountains,

distant hills powdered blue as a girl's eyelid.
It seems the least little shove would land us there,

that only the slightest repugnance of our bodies
we no longer control could drag us back.

Buenos Aires

In my room at the Hotel Continentál
a thousand miles from nowhere,
I heard
the bulky, beefy breathing of the herds.

Cattle furnished my new clothes:
my coat of limp, chestnut-colored suede,
my sharp shoes
that hurt my toes.

A false fin de siècle decorum
snored over Buenos Aires
lost in the pampas
and run by the barracks.

All day I read about newspaper coups d'état
of the leaden, internecine generals—
lumps of dough on the chessboard—and never saw
their countermarching tanks.

Along the sunlit cypress walks
of the Republican martyrs' graveyard,
hundreds of one-room Roman temples
hugged their neo-classical catafalques.

Literal commemorative busts
preserved the frogged coats
and fussy, furrowed foreheads
of those soldier bureaucrats.

By their brazen doors
a hundred marble goddesses
wept like willows. I found rest
by cupping a soft palm to each hard breast.

I was the worse for wear,
and my breath whitened the winter air
next morning, when Buenos Aires filled
with frowning, starch-collared crowds.

Soft Wood

[FOR HARRIET WINSLOW]

Sometimes I have supposed seals
must live as long as the Scholar Gypsy.
Even in their barred pond at the zoo they are happy,
and no sunflower turns
more delicately to the sun
without a wincing of the will.

Here too in Maine things bend to the wind forever.
After two years away, one must get used
to the painted soft wood staying bright and clean,
to the air blasting an all-white wall whiter,
as it blows through curtain and screen
touched with salt and evergreen.

The green juniper berry spills crystal-clear gin,
and even the hot water in the bathtub
is more than water,
and rich with the scouring effervescence
of something healing,
the illimitable salt.

Things last, but sometimes for days here
only children seem fit to handle children,
and there is no utility or inspiration
in the wind smashing without direction.
The fresh paint
on the captains' houses hides softer wood.

Their square-riggers used to whiten
the four corners of the globe,
but it's no consolation to know
the possessors seldom outlast the possessions,
once warped and mothered by their touch.
Shed skin will never fit another wearer.

Yet the seal pack will bark past my window
summer after summer.
This is the season
when our friends may and will die daily.
Surely the lives of the old
are briefer than the young.

Harriet Winslow, who owned this house,
was more to me than my mother.
I think of you far off in Washington,
breathing in the heat wave
and air-conditioning, knowing
each drug that numbs alerts another nerve to pain.

New York 1962: Fragment

[FOR E.H.L.]

This might be nature—twenty stories high,
two water tanks, tanned shingle, corseted
by stapled pasture wire, while bed to bed,
we two, one cell here, lie
gazing into the ether's crystal ball,
sky and a sky, and sky, and sky, till death—
my heart stops . . .
This might be heaven. Years ago,
we aimed for less and settled for
a picture, out of style then and now in,
of seven daffodils. We watched them blow:
buttercup yellow were the flowers, and green
the stems as fresh paint, over them the wind,
the blousy wooden branches of the elms,
high summer in the breath that overwhelms
the termites digging in the underpinning . . .
Still over us, still in parenthesis,
this sack of hornets sopping up the flame,
still over us our breath,
sawing and pumping to the terminal,
and down below, we two, two in one waterdrop
vitalized by a needle drop of blood,
up, up, up, up and up,
soon shot, soon slugged into the overflow
that sets the wooden workhorse working here below.

The Flaw

A seal swims like a poodle through the sheet
of blinding salt. A country graveyard, here
and there a rock, and here and there a pine,
throbs on the essence of the gasoline.
Some mote, some eye-flaw, wobbles in the heat,
hair-thin, hair-dark, the fragment of a hair—

a noose, a question? All is possible;
if there's free will, it's something like this hair,
inside my eye, outside my eye, yet free,
airless as grace, if the good God . . . I see.
Our bodies quiver. In this rustling air,
all's possible, all's unpredictable.

Old wives and husbands! Look, their gravestones wait
in couples with the names and half the date—
one future and one freedom. In a flash,
I see us whiten into skeletons,
our eager, sharpened cries, a pair of stones,
cutting like shark-fins through the boundless wash.

Two walking cobwebs, almost bodiless,
crossed paths here once, kept house, and lay in beds.
Your fingertips once touched my fingertips
and set us tingling through a thousand threads.
Poor pulsing *Fête Champêtre!* The summer slips
between our fingers into nothingness.

We too lean forward, as the heat waves roll
over our bodies, grown insensible,
ready to dwindle off into the soul,
two motes or eye-flaws, the invisible . . .
Hope of the hopeless launched and cast adrift
on the great flaw that gives the final gift.

Dear Figure curving like a questionmark,
how will you hear my answer in the dark?

Night Sweat

Work-table, litter, books and standing lamp,
plain things, my stalled equipment, the old broom—
but I am living in a tidied room,
for ten nights now I've felt the creeping damp
float over my pajamas' wilted white . . .
Sweet salt embalms me and my head is wet,
everything streams and tells me this is right;
my life's fever is soaking in night sweat—
one life, one writing! But the downward glide
and bias of existing wrings us dry—
always inside me is the child who died,
always inside me is his will to die—
one universe, one body . . . in this urn
the animal night sweats of the spirit burn.
Behind me! You! Again I feel the light
lighten my leaded eyelids, while the gray
skulled horses whinny for the soot of night.
I dabble in the dapple of the day,
a heap of wet clothes, seamy, shivering,
I see my flesh and bedding washed with light,
my child exploding into dynamite,
my wife . . . your lightness alters everything,
and tears the black web from the spider's sack,
as your heart hops and flutters like a hare.
Poor turtle, tortoise, if I cannot clear
the surface of these troubled waters here,
absolve me, help me, Dear Heart, as you bear
this world's dead weight and cycle on your back.

For the Union Dead

"Relinquunt Omnia Servare Rem Publicam."

The old South Boston Aquarium stands
in a Sahara of snow now. Its broken windows are boarded.
The bronze weathervane cod has lost half its scales.
The airy tanks are dry.

Once my nose crawled like a snail on the glass;
my hand tingled
to burst the bubbles
drifting from the noses of the cowed, compliant fish.

My hand draws back. I often sigh still
for the dark downward and vegetating kingdom
of the fish and reptile. One morning last March,
I pressed against the new barbed and galvanized

fence on the Boston Common. Behind their cage,
yellow dinosaur steamshovels were grunting
as they cropped up tons of mush and grass
to gouge their underworld garage.

Parking spaces luxuriate like civic
sandpiles in the heart of Boston.
A girdle of orange, Puritan-pumpkin colored girders
braces the tingling Statehouse,

shaking over the excavations, as it faces Colonel Shaw
and his bell-cheeked Negro infantry
on St. Gaudens' shaking Civil War relief,
propped by a plank splint against the garage's earthquake.

Two months after marching through Boston,
half the regiment was dead;
at the dedication,
William James could almost hear the bronze Negroes breathe.

Their monument sticks like a fishbone
in the city's throat.
Its Colonel is as lean
as a compass-needle.

He has an angry wrenlike vigilance,
a greyhound's gentle tautness;
he seems to wince at pleasure,
and suffocate for privacy.

He is out of bounds now. He rejoices in man's lovely,
peculiar power to choose life and die—
when he leads his black soldiers to death,
he cannot bend his back.

On a thousand small town New England greens,
the old white churches hold their air
of sparse, sincere rebellion; frayed flags
quilt the graveyards of the Grand Army of the Republic.

The stone statues of the abstract Union Soldier
grow slimmer and younger each year—
wasp-waisted, they doze over muskets
and muse through their sideburns . . .

Shaw's father wanted no monument
except the ditch,
where his son's body was thrown
and lost with his "niggers."

The ditch is nearer.
There are no statues for the last war here;
on Boylston Street, a commercial photograph
shows Hiroshima boiling

over a Mosler Safe, the "Rock of Ages"
that survived the blast. Space is nearer.

When I crouch to my television set,
the drained faces of Negro school-children rise like balloons.

Colonel Shaw
is riding on his bubble,
he waits
for the blessèd break.

The Aquarium is gone. Everywhere,
giant finned cars nose forward like fish;
a savage servility
slides by on grease.

[FROM]

Near the Ocean

Near the Ocean

1. Waking Early Sunday Morning

O to break loose, like the chinook
salmon jumping and falling back,
nosing up to the impossible
stone and bone-crushing waterfall—
raw-jawed, weak-fleshed there, stopped by ten
steps of the roaring ladder, and then
to clear the top on the last try,
alive enough to spawn and die.

Stop, back off. The salmon breaks
water, and now my body wakes
to feel the unpolluted joy
and criminal leisure of a boy—
no rainbow smashing a dry fly
in the white run is free as I,
here squatting like a dragon on
time's hoard before the day's begun!

Vermin run for their unstopped holes;
in some dark nook a fieldmouse rolls
a marble, hours on end, then stops;
the termite in the woodwork sleeps—
listen, the creatures of the night
obsessive, casual, sure of foot,
go on grinding, while the sun's
daily remorseful blackout dawns.

Fierce, fireless mind, running downhill.
Look up and see the harbor fill:
business as usual in eclipse
goes down to the sea in ships—
wake of refuse, dacron rope,
bound for Bermuda or Good Hope,
all bright before the morning watch
the wine-dark hulls of yawl and ketch.

I watch a glass of water wet
with a fine fuzz of icy sweat,
silvery colors touched with sky,
serene in their neutrality—
yet if I shift, or change my mood,
I see some object made of wood,
background behind it of brown grain,
to darken it, but not to stain.

O that the spirit could remain
tinged but untarnished by its strain!
Better dressed and stacking birch,
or lost with the Faithful at Church—
anywhere, but somewhere else!
And now the new electric bells,
clearly chiming, "Faith of our fathers,"
and now the congregation gathers.

O Bible chopped and crucified
in hymns we hear but do not read,
none of the milder subtleties
of grace or art will sweeten these
stiff quatrains shoveled out four-square—
they sing of peace, and preach despair;
yet they gave darkness some control,
and left a loophole for the soul.

No, put old clothes on, and explore
the corners of the woodshed for
its dregs and dreck: tools with no handle,
ten candle-ends not worth a candle,
old lumber banished from the Temple,
damned by Paul's precept and example,
cast from the kingdom, banned in Israel,
the wordless sign, the tinkling cymbal.

When will we see Him face to face?
Each day, He shines through darker glass.
In this small town where everything
is known, I see His vanishing
emblems, His white spire and flag-
pole sticking out above the fog,
like old white china doorknobs, sad,
slight, useless things to calm the mad.

Hammering military splendor,
top-heavy Goliath in full armor—
little redemption in the mass
liquidations of their brass,
elephant and phalanx moving
with the times and still improving,
when that kingdom hit the crash:
a million foreskins stacked like trash . . .

Sing softer! But what if a new
diminuendo brings no true
tenderness, only restlessness,
excess, the hunger for success,
sanity of self-deception
fixed and kicked by reckless caution,
while we listen to the bells—
anywhere, but somewhere else!

O to break loose. All life's grandeur
is something with a girl in summer . . .
elated as the President
girdled by his establishment
this Sunday morning, free to chaff
his own thoughts with his bear-cuffed staff,
swimming nude, unbuttoned, sick
of his ghost-written rhetoric!

No weekends for the gods now. Wars
flicker, earth licks its open sores,
fresh breakage, fresh promotions, chance
assassinations, no advance.
Only man thinning out his kind
sounds through the Sabbath noon, the blind
swipe of the pruner and his knife
busy about the tree of life . . .

Pity the planet, all joy gone
from this sweet volcanic cone;
peace to our children when they fall
in small war on the heels of small
war—until the end of time
to police the earth, a ghost
orbiting forever lost
in our monotonous sublime.

2. Fourth of July in Maine

[FOR HARRIET WINSLOW]

Another summer! Our Independence
Day Parade, all innocence
of children's costumes, helps resist
the communist and socialist.
Five nations: Dutch, French, Englishmen,
Indians, and we, who held Castine,
rise from their graves in combat gear—
world-losers elsewhere, conquerors here!

Civil Rights clergy face again
the scions of the good old strain,
the poor who always must remain
poor and Republicans in Maine,
upholders of the American Dream,
who will not sink and cannot swim—
Emersonian self-reliance,
lethargy of Russian peasants!

High noon. Each child has won his blue,
red, yellow ribbon, and our statue,
a dandyish Union Soldier, sees
his fields reclaimed by views and spruce—
he seems a convert to old age,
small, callous, elbowed off the stage,
while the canned martial music fades
from scene and green—no more parades!

Blue twinges of mortality
remind us the theocracy
drove in its stakes here to command
the infinite, and gave this land
a ministry that would have made
short work of Christ, the Son of God,
and then exchanged His crucifix,
hardly our sign, for politics.

This white Colonial frame house,
willed downward, Dear, from you to us,
still matters—the Americas'
best artifact produced en masse.
The founders' faith was in decay,
and yet their building seems to say:
"Every time I take a breath,
my God you are the air I breathe."

New England, everywhere I look,
old letters crumble from the Book,
China trade rubble, one more line
unravelling from the dark design
spun by God and Cotton Mather—
our *bel età dell' oro*, another
bright thing thinner than a cobweb,
caught in Calvinism's ebb.

Dear Cousin, life is much the same,
though only fossils know your name
here since you left this solitude,
gone, as the Christians say, for good.
Your house, still outwardly in form
lasts, though no emissary come
to watch the garden running down,
or photograph the propped-up barn.

If memory is genius, you
had Homer's, enough gossip to
repeople Trollope's Barchester,
nurses, Negro, diplomat, down-easter,
cousins kept up with, nipped, corrected,
kindly, majorfully directed,
though family furniture, decor,
and rooms redone meant almost more.

How often when the telephone
brought you to us from Washington,
we had to look around the room
to find the objects you would name—
lying there, ten years paralyzed,
half blind, no voice unrecognized,
not trusting in the afterlife,
teasing us for a carving knife.

High New England summer, warm
and fortified against the storm
by nightly nips you once adored,
though never going overboard,
Harriet, when you used to play
your chosen Nadia Boulanger
Monteverdi, Purcell, and Bach's
precursors on the Magnavox.

Blue-ribboned, blue-jeaned, named for you,
our daughter cartwheels on the blue—
may your proportion strengthen her
to live through the millennial year
Two Thousand, and like you possess
friends, independence, and a house,
herself God's plenty, mistress of
your tireless sedentary love.

Her two angora guinea pigs
are nibbling seed, the news, and twigs—
untroubled, petrified, atremble,
a mother and her daughter, so humble,
giving, idle and sensitive,
few animals will let them live,
and only a vegetarian God
could look on them and call them good.

Man's poorest cousins, harmonies
of lust and appetite and ease,
little pacific things, who graze
the grass about their box, they praise
whatever stupor gave them breath
to multiply before their death—
Evolution's snails, by birth,
outrunning man who runs the earth.

And now the frosted summer night-dew
brightens, the north wind rushes through
your ailing cedars, finds the gaps;
thumbtacks rattle from the white maps,
food's lost sight of, dinner waits,
in the cold oven, icy plates—
repeating and repeating, one
Joan Baez on the gramophone.

And here in your converted barn,
we burn our hands a moment, borne
by energies that never tire
of piling fuel on the fire;
monologue that will not hear,
logic turning its deaf ear,
wild spirits and old sores in league
with inexhaustible fatigue.

Far off that time of gentleness,
when man, still licensed to increase,
unfallen and unmated, heard
only the uncreated Word—
when God the Logos still had wit
to hide his bloody hands, and sit
in silence, while his peace was sung.
Then the universe was young.

We watch the logs fall. Fire once gone,
we're done for: we escape the sun,
rising and setting, a red coal,
until it cinders like the soul.
Great ash and sun of freedom, give
us this day the warmth to live,
and face the household fire. We turn
our backs, and feel the whiskey burn.

3. The Opposite House

All day the opposite house,
an abandoned police stable,
just an opposite house,
is square enough—six floors,
six windows to a floor,
pigeons ganging through
broken windows and cooing
like gangs of children tooting
empty bottles.

Tonight, though, I see it shine
in the Azores of my open window.
Its manly, old-fashioned lines
are gorgeously rectilinear.
It's like some firework to be fired
at the end of the garden party,
some Spanish *casa*, luminous
with heraldry and murder,
marooned in New York.

A stringy policeman is crooked
in the doorway, one hand on his revolver.
He counts his bullets like beads.
Two on horseback sidle
the crowd to the curb. A red light
whirls on the roof of an armed car,
plodding slower than a turtle.
Deterrent terror!
Viva la muerte!

4. Central Park

Scaling small rocks, exhaling smog,
gasping at game-scents like a dog,
now light as pollen, now as white
and winded as a grounded kite—
I watched the lovers occupy
every inch of earth and sky:
one figure of geometry,
multiplied to infinity,
straps down, and sunning openly . . .
each precious, public, pubic tangle
an equilateral triangle,
lost in the park, half covered by
the shade of some low stone or tree.
The stain of fear and poverty
spread through each trapped anatomy,
and darkened every mote of dust.
All wished to leave this drying crust,
borne on the delicate wings of lust
like bees, and cast their fertile drop
into the overwhelming cup.

Drugged and humbled by the smell
of zoo-straw mixed with animal,
the lion prowled his slummy cell,
serving his life-term in jail—
glaring, grinding, on his heel,
with tingling step and testicle . . .

Behind a dripping rock, I found
a one-day kitten on the ground—
deprived, weak, ignorant and blind,
squeaking, tubular, left behind—
dying with its deserter's rich
Welfare lying out of reach:
milk cartons, kidney heaped to spoil,
two plates sheathed with silver foil.

Shadows had stained the afternoon;
high in an elm, a snagged balloon
wooed the attraction of the moon.
Scurrying from the mouth of night,
a single, fluttery, paper kite
grazed Cleopatra's Needle, and sailed
where the light of the sun had failed.
Then night, the night—the jungle hour,
the rich in his slit-windowed tower . . .
Old Pharaohs starving in your foxholes,
with painted banquets on the walls,
fists knotted in your captives' hair,
tyrants with little food to spare—
all your embalming left you mortal,
glazed, black, and hideously eternal,
all your plunder and gold leaf
only served to draw the thief . . .

We beg delinquents for our life.
Behind each bush, perhaps a knife;
each landscaped crag, each flowering shrub,
hides a policeman with a club.

5. Near the Ocean

[FOR E.H.L.]

The house is filled. The last heartthrob
thrills through her flesh. The hero stands,
stunned by the applauding hands,
and lifts her once head to please the mob . . .
No, young and starry-eyed, the brother
and sister wait before their mother,
old iron-bruises, powder, "Child,
these breasts . . ." He knows. And if she's killed

his treadmill heart will never rest—
his wet mouth pressed to some slack breast,
or shifting over on his back . . .
The severed radiance filters back,
athirst for nightlife—gorgon head,
fished up from the Aegean dead,
with all its stranded snakes uncoiled,
here beheaded and despoiled.

We hear the ocean. Older seas
and deserts give asylum, peace
to each abortion and mistake.
Lost in the Near Eastern dreck,
the tyrant and tyrannicide
lie like the bridegroom and the bride;
the battering ram, abandoned, prone,
beside the apeman's phallic stone.

Betrayals! Was it the first night?
They stood against a black and white
inland New England backdrop. No dogs
there, horse or hunter, only frogs
chirring from the dark trees and swamps.
Elms watching like extinguished lamps.
Knee-high hedges of black sheep
encircling them at every step.

Some subway-green coldwater flat,
its walls tattooed with neon light,
then high delirious squalor, food
burned down with vodka . . . menstrual blood
caking the covers, when they woke
to the dry, childless Sunday walk,
saw cars on Brooklyn Bridge descend
through steel and coal dust to land's end.

Was it years later when they met,
and summer's coarse last-quarter drought
had dried the hardveined elms to bark—
lying like people out of work,
dead sober, cured, recovered, on
the downslope of some gritty green,
all access barred with broken glass;
and dehydration browned the grass?

Is it this shore? Their eyes worn white
as moons from hitting bottom? Night,
the sandfleas scissoring their feet,
the sandbed cooling to concrete,
one borrowed blanket, lights of cars
shining down at them like stars? . . .
Sand built the lost Atlantis . . . sand,
Atlantic Ocean, condoms, sand.

Sleep, sleep. The ocean, grinding stones,
can only speak the present tense;
nothing will age, nothing will last,
or take corruption from the past.
A hand, your hand then! I'm afraid
to touch the crisp hair on your head—
Monster loved for what you are,
till time, that buries us, lay bare.

[FROM]

History

History

History has to live with what was here,
clutching and close to fumbling all we had—
it is so dull and gruesome how we die,
unlike writing, life never finishes.
Abel was finished; death is not remote,
a flash-in-the-pan electrifies the skeptic,
his cows crowding like skulls against high-voltage wire,
his baby crying all night like a new machine.
As in our Bibles, white-faced, predatory,
the beautiful, mist-drunken hunter's moon ascends—
a child could give it a face: two holes, two holes,
my eyes, my mouth, between them a skull's no-nose—
O there's a terrifying innocence in my face
drenched with the silver salvage of the mornfrost.

Man and Woman

The sheep start galloping in moon-blind wheels
shedding a dozen ewes—is it faulty vision?
Will we get them back . . . and everything,
marriage and departure, departure and marriage,
village to family, family to village—
all the sheep's parents in geometric progression?
It's too much heart-ache to go back to that—
not life-enhancing like the hour a student
first discovers the authentic Mother
on the Tuscan hills of Berenson,
or of Galileo, his great glass eye
admiring the spots on the erroneous moon. . . .
I watch this night out grateful to be alone
with my wife—your slow pulse, my outrageous eye.

Alexander

His sweet moist eye missed nothing—the vague guerrilla,
new ground, new tactics, the time for his hell-fire drive,
Demosthenes knotting his nets of dialectic—
phalanxes oiled ten weeks before their trial,
engines on oxen for the fall of Tyre—
Achilles . . . in Aristotle's annotated copy—
health burning like the dewdrop on his flesh
hit in a hundred calculated sallies
to give the Persians the cup of love, of brothers—
the wine-bowl of the Macedonian drinking bout . . .
drinking out of friendship, then meeting Medius,
then drinking, then bathing, then sleeping, then meeting Medius,
then drinking, then bathing . . . dead at thirty-two—
in this life only is our hope in Christ.

Death of Alexander

The young man's numinous eye is like the sun,
for three days the Macedonian soldiers pass;
speechless, he knows them as if they were his sheep.
Shall Alexander be carried in the temple
to pray there, and perhaps, recover? But
the god forbids it, "It's a better thing
if the king stay where he is." He soon dies,
this after all, perhaps, the "better thing." . . .
No one was like him. Terrible were his crimes—
but if you wish to blackguard the Great King,
think how mean, obscure and dull you are,
your labors lowly and your merits less—
we know this, of all the kings of old,
he alone had the greatness of heart to repent.

Marcus Cato 234–149 B.C.

My live telephone swings crippled to solitude
two feet from my ear; as so often and so often,
I hold your dialogue away to breathe—
still this is love, Old Cato forgoing his wife,
then jumping her in thunderstorms like *Juppiter Tonans;*
his forthrightness gave him long days of solitude,
then deafness changed his gifts for rule to genius:
Cato knew from the Greeks that empire is hurry,
and dominion never goes to the phlegmatic—
it was hard to be Demosthenes in his stone-deaf Senate:
"Carthage must die," he roared . . . and Carthage died.
He knew a blindman looking for gold
in a heap of dust must take the dust with the gold,
Rome, if built at all, must be built in a day.

Marcus Cato 95–42 B.C.

As a boy he was brought to Sulla's villa, The Tombs,
saw people come in as men, and leave as heads.
"Why hasn't someone killed him?" he asked. They answered,
"Men fear Sulla even more than they hate him."
He asked for a sword, and wasn't invited back . . .
He drowned Plato in wine all night with his friends,
gambled his life in the forum, was stoned like Paul,
and went on talking till soldiers saved the State,
saved Caesar. . . . At the last cast of his lost Republic,
he bloodied his hand on the slave who hid his sword;
he fell in a small sleep, heard the dawn birds chirping,
but couldn't use his hand well . . . when they tried to put
his bowels back, he tore them . . . He's where he would be:
one Roman who died, perhaps, for Rome.

Cicero, the Sacrificial Killing

It's somewhere, somewhere, thought beats stupidly—
a scarlet patch of Tacitus or the Bible,
Pound's Cantos lost in the rockslide of history?
The great man flees his greatness, fugitive husk
of Cicero or Marius without a toga,
old sheep sent out to bite the frosty stubble.
The Republic froze and fattened its high ranks,
the Empire was too much brass for what we are;
who asks for legions to bring the baby milk?
Cicero bold, garrulous in his den
chatting as host on his sofa of magazines;
a squad of state doctors stands by him winking . . .
he minds his hands shaking, and they keep shaking;
if infirmity has a color, it isn't yellow.

Nunc est bibendum, Cleopatra's Death

Nunc est bibendum, nunc pede liberum
the time to drink and dance the earth in rhythm.
Before this it was infamous to banquet,
while Cleopatra plotted to enthrone
her depravity naked in the Capitol—
impotent, yet drunk on fortune's favors!
Caesar has tamed your soul, you see with a
now sober eye the scowling truth of terror—
O Cleopatra scarcely escaping with a single ship
Caesar, three decks of oars—O scarcely escaping
when the sparrowhawk falls on the soft-textured dove. . . .
You found a more magnanimous way to die,
not walking on foot in triumphant Caesar's triumph,
no queen now, but a private woman much humbled.

Attila, Hitler

Hitler had fingertips of apprehension,
"Who knows how long I'll live? Let us have war.
We *are* the barbarians, the world is near the end."
Attila mounted on raw meat and greens
galloped to massacre in his single fieldmouse suit,
he never left a house that wasn't burning,
could only sleep on horseback, sinking deep
in his rural dream. Would he have found himself
in this coarsest, cruelest, least magnanimous,
most systematic, most philosophical . . .
a nomad stay-at-home: *He who has, has;*
a barbarian wondering why the old world collapsed,
who also left his festering fume of refuse,
old tins, dead vermin, ashes, eggshells, youth?

Mohammed

Like Henry VIII, Mohammed got religion
in the dangerous years, and smashed the celibates,
haters of life, though never takers of it—
changed their monasteries to foundries,
reset their non-activist Buddhistic rote
to the *schrecklichkeit* and warsongs of his tribe.
The Pope still twangs his harp for chastity—
the boys of the jihad on a string of unwitting camels
rush paradise, halls stocked with adolescent
beauties, both sexes for simple nomad tastes—
how warmly they sleep in tile-abstraction alcoves;
love is resurrection, and her war a rose:
woman wants man, man woman, as naturally
as the thirsty frog desires the rain.

Death of Count Roland

King Marsilius of Saragossa
does not love God, he is carried to the shade of the orchard,
and sits reclining on his bench of blue tile,
with more than twenty thousand men about him;
his speech is only the one all kings must make,
it did to spark the Franco-Moorish War. . . .
At war's end Roland's brains seeped from his ears;
he called for the Angel Michael, his ivory horn,
prayed for his peers, and scythed his sword, Durendal—
farther away than a man might shoot a crossbow,
toward Saragossa, there is a grassy place,
Roland went to it, climbed the little mound:
a beautiful tree there, four great stones of marble—
on the green grass, he has fallen back, has fainted.

Joinville and Louis IX

"Given my pilgrim's scarf and staff, I left
the village of Joinville on foot, barefoot, in my shirt,
never turning my eyes for fear my heart would melt
at leaving my mortgaged castle, my two fair children—
a Crusader? Some of us were, and lived to be ransomed.
Bishops, nobles, and Brothers of the King
strolled free in Acre, and begged the King to sail home,
and leave the meaner folk. Sore of heart then,
I went to a barred window, and passed my arms through the bars
of the window, and someone came, and leant on my shoulders,
and placed his two hands on my forehead—Philip de Nemours?
I screamed, 'Leave me in peace!' His hand dropped by chance,
and I knew the King by the emerald on his finger:
'If I should leave Jerusalem, who will remain?' "

Dante 3. Buonconte

"No one prays for me . . . Giovanna or the others."
What took you so far from Campaldino
we never found your body? "Where the Archiano
at the base of the Casentino loses its name
and becomes the Arno, I stopped running,
the war lost, and wounded in the throat—
flying on foot and splashing the field with blood.
There I lost sight and speech, and died saying *Maria*. . . .
I'll tell you the truth, tell it to the living,
an angel and devil fought with claws for my soul:
You angel, why do you rob me for his last word?
The rain fell, then the hail, my body froze,
until the raging Archiano snatched me,
and loosened my arms I'd folded like the cross."

Dames du Temps jadis

Say in what country, where
is Flora, the Roman,
Archipaida or Thais
far lovelier,
or Echo whose voice would answer
across the land or river—
her beauty more than human.
Where is our wise Eloise
and Peter Abelard
gelded at Saint Denis
for love of her—
Jehanne the good maid of Lorraine
the English burned at Rouen?
Where, mother of God, is last year's snow?

Coleridge and Richard II

Coleridge wasn't flatter-blinded by
his kinship with Richard II . . . a *feminine friendism*,
the constant overflow of imagination
proportioned to his dwindling will to act.
Richard unkinged saw shipwreck in the mirror,
not the King; womanlike, he feared
he must see himself more frequently to exist,
the white glittering inertia of the iceberg.
Coleridge had the cheering fancy only blacks
would cherish slavery for two thousand years;
though most negroes in 1800 London were
onwardlooking and further exiled
from the jungle of dead kings than Coleridge,
the one poet who blamed his failure on himself.

Bosworth Field

In a minute, two inches of rain stream through my dry
garden stones, clear as crystal, without trout—
we have gone down and down, gone the wrong brook.
Robespierre and Stalin mostly killed people they knew,
Richard the Third was Dickon, Duke of Gloucester,
long arm of the realm, goddam blood royal,
terrible underpinning of what he let breathe.
No wonder, we have dug him up past proof,
still fighting drunk on mortal wounds,
ready to gallop down his own apologist.
What does he care for Thomas More and Shakespeare
pointing fingers at his polio'd body;
for the moment, he is king; he is the king
saying: *it's better to have lived, than live.*

Sir Thomas More

Holbein's More, my patron saint as a convert,
the gold chain of S's, the golden rose,
the plush cap, the brow's damp feathertips of hair,
the good eyes' stern, facetious twinkle, ready
to turn from executioner to martyr—
or saunter with the great King's bluff arm on your neck,
feeling that friend-slaying, terror-dazzled heart
ballooning off into its awful dream—
a noble saying, "How the King must love you!"
And you, "If it were a question of my head,
or losing his meanest village in France . . ."
then by the scaffold and the headsman's axe—
"Friend, give me your hand for the first step,
as for coming down, I'll shift for myself."

Death of Anne Boleyn

Summer hail flings crystals on the window—
they wrapped the Lady Ann's head in a white handker-
    chief. . . .
To Wolsey, *the nightcrow*, but to Anthony Froude,
stoic virtue spoke from her stubborn lips and chin—
five adulteries in three years of marriage;
the game was hotly charged. "I hear say I'll
not die till noon; I am very sorry therefore,
I thought to be dead this hour and past my pain."
Her jailer told her that beheading was no pain—
"It is subtle." "I have a little neck,"
she said, and put her hands about it laughing.
They guessed she had much pleasure and joy in death—
no foreigners admitted. By the King's abundance
the scene was open to any Englishman.

Charles V by Titian

But we cannot go back to Charles V
barreled in armor, more gold fleece than king;
he haws on the gristle of a Flemish word,
his upper and lower Hapsburg jaws won't meet.
The sunset he tilts at is big Venetian stuff,
the true Charles, done by Titian, never lived.
The battle he rides offstage to is offstage.
No St. Francis, he did what Francis shied at,
gave up office, one of twenty monarchs
since Saturn who willingly made the grand refusal.
In his burgherish monastery, he learned he couldn't
put together a clock with missing parts.
He had dreamed of a democracy of Europe,
and carried enemies with him in a cage.

Marlowe

Vain surety of man's mind so near to death,
twenty-nine years with hopes to total fifty—
one blurred, hurried, still undecoded month
hurled Marlowe from England to his companion shades.
His mighty line denies his shady murder:
"How uncontrollably sweet and swift my life
with two London hits and riding my high tide,
drinking out May in Deptford with three friends,
one or all four perhaps in Secret Service.
Christ was a bastard, His Testament's filthily Greeked—
I died swearing, stabbed with friends who knew me—
was it the bar-check? . . . Tragedy is to die . . .
for that vacant parsonage, Posterity;
my plays are stamped in bronze, my life in tabloid."

Mary Stuart

They ran for their lives up nightslope, gained the car,
the girl's maxi-coat, Tsar officer's, dragged the snow,
she and he killed her husband, they stained the snow.
Romance of the snowflakes! Men swam up the night,
grass pike in overalls with scythe and pitchfork;
shouting, "Take the car, we'll smash the girl."
Once kings were on firstname terms with the poor,
a car was a castle, and money belonged to the rich. . . .
They roared off hell-wheel and scattered the weak mob;
happily only one man splashed the windshield,
they dared not pluck him, it was hard at night
to hold to the road with a carcass on the windshield—
at nightmare's end, the bedroom, dark night of marriage,
the bloodiest hands were joined and took no blood.

Rembrandt

His faces crack . . . if mine could crack and breathe!
His Jewish Bridegroom, hand spread on the Jewish Bride's
bashful, tapestried, level bosom, is faithful;
the fair girl, poor background, gives soul to his flayed steer.
Her breasts, the snowdrops, have lasted out the storm.
Often the Dutch were sacks, their women sacks,
the obstinate, undefeated hull of an old scow;
but Bathsheba's ample stomach, her heavy, practical feet,
are reverently dried by the faithful servant,
his eyes dwell lovingly on each fulfilled sag;
her unfortunate body is the privilege of service,
is radiant with an homage void of possession. . . .
We see, if we see at all, through a copper mist
the strange new idol for the marketplace.

The Worst Sinner, Jonathan Edwards' God

The earliest sportsman in the earliest dawn,
waking to what redness, waking a killer,
saw the red cane was sweet in his red grip;
the blood of the shepherd matched the blood of the wolf.
But Jonathan Edwards prayed to think himself
worse than any man that ever breathed;
he was a good man, and he prayed with reason—
which of us hasn't thought his same thought worse?
Each night I lie me down to heal in sleep;
two or three mornings a week, I wake to my sin—
sins, not sin; not two or three mornings, seven.
God himself cannot wake five years younger,
and drink away the venom in the chalice—
the best man in the best world possible.

Watchmaker God

Say life is the one-way trip, the one-way flight,
say this without hysterical undertones—
then you could say you stood in the cold light of science,
seeing as you are seen, espoused to fact.
Strange, life is both the fire and fuel; and we,
the animals and objects, must be here
without striking a spark of evidence
that anything that ever stopped living
ever falls back to living when life stops.
There's a pale romance to the watchmaker God
of Descartes and Paley; He drafted and installed
us in the Apparatus. He loved to tinker;
but having perfected what He had to do,
stood off shrouded in his loneliness.

Robespierre and Mozart as Stage

Robespierre could live with himself: "The republic
of Virtue without *la terreur* is a disaster.
Loot the châteaux, give bread to Saint Antoine."
He found the guillotine was not an idler
hearing *mort à Robespierre* from the Convention floor,
the high harsh laughter of the innocents,
the Revolution returning to grand tragedy—
is life the place where we find happiness,
or not at all? . . . Ask the voyeur
what blue movie is worth a seat at the keyhole. . . .
Even the prompted Louis Seize was living theater,
sternly and lovingly judged by his critics, who knew
a Mozart's insolent slash at folk could never
cut the gold thread of the suffocating curtain.

Saint-Just 1767–93

Saint-Just: his name seems stolen from the Missal. . . .
His chamois coat, the dandy's vast cravat
knotted with pretentious negligence;
he carried his head like the Holy Sacrament.
He thought only the laconic fit to rule
the austerity of his hideous cardboard Sparta.
"I shall move with the stone footsteps of the sun—
faction plagues the ebb of revolution,
as reptiles follow the dry bed of a torrent.
I am young and therefore close to nature.
Happiness is a new idea in Europe;
we bronzed liberty with the guillotine.
I'm still twenty, I've done badly, I'll do better."
He did, the scaffold, "Je sais où je vais."

Napoleon

Boston's used bookshops, anachronisms from London,
are gone; it's hard to guess now why I spent
my vacations lugging home his third-hand *Lives*—
shaking the dust from that stationary stock:
cheap deluxe lithographs and gilt-edged pulp
on a man . . . not bloodthirsty, not sparing of blood,
with an eye and *sang-froid* to manage everything;
his iron hand no mere appendage of his mind
for improbable contingencies . . .
for uprooting races, lineages, Jacobins—
the price was paltry . . . three million soldiers dead,
grand opera fixed like morphine in their veins.
Dare we say, he had no moral center?
All gone like the smoke of his own artillery?

Waterloo

A thundercloud hung on the mantel of our summer
cottage by the owners, Miss Barnard and Mrs. Curtis:
a sad picture, half life-scale, removed and no doubt
scrapped as too English Empire for our taste:
Waterloo, Waterloo! You could choose sides then:
the engraving made the blue French uniforms black,
the British Redcoats gray; those running were French—
an aide-de-camp, Napoleon's perhaps,
wore a cascade of overstated braid,
there sabered, dying, his standard wrenched from weak hands;
his killer, a bonneted fog-gray dragoon—
six centuries, this field of their encounter,
death-round of French sex against the English *no* . . .
La Gloire fading to *sauve qui peut* and *merde*.

Beethoven

Our cookbook is bound like Whitman's *Leaves of Grass*—
gold title on green. I have escaped its death,
take two eggs with butter, drink and smoke;
I live past prudence, not possibility—
who can banquet on the shifting cloud,
lie to friends and tell the truth in print,
be Othello offstage, or Lincoln retired from office?
The vogue of the vague, what can it teach an artist?
Beethoven was a Romantic, but too good;
did kings, republics or Napoleon teach him?
He was his own Napoleon. Did even deafness?
Does the painted soldier in the painting bleed?
Is the captive chorus of *Fidelio* bound?
For a good voice hearing is a torture.

The Lost Tune

As I grow older, I must admit with terror:
I have been there, the works of the masters lose,
songs with a mind, philosophy that danced.
Their *vivace* clogs, I am too tired, or wise.
I have read in books that even woman dies;
a figure cracks up sooner than a landscape—
your subject was Maine, a black and white engraving,
able to enlarge the formal luxury of
foliage rendered by a microscope,
a thousand blueberry bushes marching up
the flank of a hill; the artist, a lady, shoots
her lover panting like a stag at bay;
not very true, yet art—had Schubert scored it,
and his singer left the greenroom with her voice.

Coleridge

Coleridge stands, he flamed for the one friend. . . .
This shower is warm, I almost breathe-in the rain
horseclopping from fire escape to skylight
down to a dungeon courtyard. In April, New York
has a smell and taste of life. For whom . . . what?
A newer younger generation faces
the firing squad, then their blood is wiped from the
    pavement. . . .
Coleridge's laudanum and brandy,
his alderman's stroll to positive negation—
his passive courage is paralysis,
standing him upright like tenpins for the strike,
only kept standing by a hundred scared habits . . .
a large soft-textured plant with pith within,
power without strength, an involuntary imposter.

Margaret Fuller Drowned

You had everything to rattle the men who wrote.
The first American woman? Margaret Fuller . . .
in a white nightgown, your hair fallen long
at the foot of the foremast, you just forty,
your husband Angelo thirty, your Angelino one—
all drowned with brief anguish together. . . . Your fire-call,
your voice, was like thorns crackling under a pot,
you knew the Church burdens and infects as all dead forms,
however gallant and lovely in their life;
progress is not by renunciation.
"Myself," you wrote, "is all I know of heaven.
With my intellect, I always can
and always shall make out, but that's not half—
the life, the life, O my God, will life never be sweet?"

Abraham Lincoln

All day I bang and bang at you in thought,
as if I had the license of your wife. . . .
If War is the continuation of politics—
is politics the discontinuation of murder?
You may have loved underdogs and even mankind,
this one thing made you different from your equals . . .
you, our one genius in politics . . . who followed
the bull to the altar . . . to death in unity.
J'accuse, j'accuse, j'accuse, j'accuse, j'accuse!
Say it in American. Who shot the deserters?
Winter blows sparks in the face of the new God,
who breathes-in fire and dies with cooling faith,
as the firebrand turns black in the black hand,
and the squealing pig darts sidewise from his foot.

Verdun

I bow down to the great goiter of Verdun,
I know what's buried there, ivory telephone,
ribs, hips bleached to parchment, a pale machinegun—
they lie fatigued from too much punishment,
cling by a string to friends they knew firsthand,
to the God of our fathers still twenty like themselves.
Their medals and rosettes have kept in bloom,
they stay young, only living makes us age.
I know the sort of town they came from, straight brownstone,
each house cooled by a rectilinear private garden,
a formal greeting and a slice of life.
The city says, "I am the finest city"—
landmass held by half a million bodies
for Berlin and Paris, twin cities saved at Verdun.

Serpent

"When I was changed from a feeble cosmopolite
to a fanatical antisemite,
I didn't let you chew my time with chatter,
bury my one day's reasonable explanations
in your equal verisimilitude the next. . . .
But I got to the schools, their hysterical faith
in the spoken word, hypnotic hammer blows,
indelible, ineradicable,
the politician wedded to a mind—
I come once in a blue moon. . . . I my age
its magical interpretation of the world,
enslaved to will and not intelligence. . . .
Soon it was obvious I didn't enjoy my war.
I'd no time for concerts, theater, to go to movies."

Words

Christ's first portrait was a donkey's head,
the simple truth is in his simple word,
lies buried in a random, haggard sentence,
cutting ten ways to nothing clearly carried. . . .
In our time, God is an entirely lost person—
there were two: Benito Mussolini and Hitler,
blind mouths shouting people into things.
After their Chicago deaths with girls and Lügers,
we know they gave a plot to what they planned.
No league against the ephemeral Enemy lasts;
not even the aristocracy of the Commune
curing the seven plagues of economics,
to wither daily in favor of the state,
a covenant of swords without the word.

Sunrise

There is always enough daylight in hell to blind;
the flower of what was left grew sweeter for them,
two done people conversing with bamboo fans
as if to brush the firefall from the air—
Admiral Onishi, still a cult to his juniors,
the father of the Kamikazes . . . he became a fish hawk
flying our armadas down like game;
his young pilots loved him to annihilation.
He chats in his garden, the sky is zigzag fire.
One butchery is left, his wife keeps nagging him to do it.
Husband and wife taste cup after cup of Scotch;
how garrulously they patter about their grandchildren—
when his knife goes home, it goes home wrong. . . .
For eighteen hours you died with your hand in hers.

Randall Jarrell 1. October 1965

Sixty, seventy, eighty: I would see you mellow,
unchanging grasshopper, whistling down the grass-fires;
the same hair, snow-touched, and wrist for tennis; soon doubles
not singles . . . Who dares go with you to your deadfall,
see the years wrinkling up the reservoir,
watch the ivy turning a wash of blood
on your infirmary wall? Thirty years ago,
as students waiting for Europe and spring term to end—
we saw below us, golden, small, stockstill,
the college polo field, cornfields, the feudal airdrome,
the McKinley Trust; behind, above us, the tower,
the dorms, the fieldhouse, the Bishop's palace and chapel—
Randall, the scene still plunges at the windshield,
apples redden to ripeness on the whiplash bough.

Randall Jarrell 2

I grizzle the embers of our onetime life,
our first intoxicating disenchantments,
dipping our hands once, not twice in the newness . . .
coming back to Kenyon on the Ohio local—
the view, middle distance, back and foreground, shifts,
silos shifting squares like chessmen—a wheel
turned by the water buffalo through the blue
of true space before the dawn of days . . .
Then the night of the caged squirrel on his wheel,
lights, eyes, peering at you from the overpass;
black-gloved, black-coated, you plod out stubbornly
as if in lockstep to grasp your blank not-I
at the foot of the tunnel . . . as if asleep, Child Randall,
greeting the cars, and approving—your harsh luminosity.

Randall Jarrell 3

The dream went like a rake of sliced bamboo,
slats of dust distracted by a downdraw;
I woke and knew I held a cigarette;
I looked, there was none, could have been none;
I slept off years before I woke again,
palming the floor, shaking the sheets. I saw
nothing was burning. I awoke, I saw
I was holding two lighted cigarettes . . .
They come this path, old friends, old buffs of death.
Tonight it's Randall, his spark still fire though humble,
his gnawed wrist cradled like *Kitten.* "What kept you so long,
racing the cooling grindstone of your ambition?
You didn't write, you *re*wrote . . . But tell me,
Cal, why did we live? Why do we die?"

Stalin

Winds on the stems make them creak like things of man;
a hedge of vines and bushes—three or four
kinds, grape-leaf, elephant-ear and alder,
an arabesque, imperfect and alive,
a hundred hues of green, the darkest shades
fall short of black, the whitest leaf-back short of white.
The state, if we could see behind the wall,
is woven of perishable vegetation.
Stalin? What shot him clawing up the tree of power—
millions plowed under with the crops they grew,
his intimates dying like the spider-bridegroom?
The large stomach could only chew success. What raised him
was an unusual lust to break the icon,
joke cruelly, seriously, and be himself.

William Carlos Williams

Who loved more? William Carlos Williams,
in collegiate black slacks, gabardine coat,
and loafers polished like rosewood on yachts,
straying stonefoot through his town-end garden,
man and flower seedy with three autumn strokes,
his brown, horned eyes enlarged, an ant's, through glasses;
his Mother, stonedeaf, her face a wizened talon,
her hair the burnt-out ash of lush Puerto Rican grass;
her black, blind, bituminous eye inquisitorial.
"Mama," he says, "which would you rather see here,
me or two blondes?" Then later, "The old bitch
is over a hundred, I'll kick off tomorrow."
He said, "I am sixty-seven, and more
attractive to girls than when I was seventeen."

Robert Frost

Robert Frost at midnight, the audience gone
to vapor, the great act laid on the shelf in mothballs,
his voice is musical and raw—he writes in the flyleaf:
For Robert from Robert, his friend in the art.
"Sometimes I feel too full of myself," I say.
And he, misunderstanding, "When I am low,
I stray away. My son wasn't your kind. The night
we told him Merrill Moore would come to treat him,
he said, 'I'll kill him first.' One of my daughters thought things,
thought every male she met was out to make her;
the way she dressed, she couldn't make a whorehouse."
And I, "Sometimes I'm so happy I can't stand myself."
And he, "When I am too full of joy, I think
how little good my health did anyone near me."

The March 1

[FOR DWIGHT MACDONALD]

Under the too white marmoreal Lincoln Memorial,
the too tall marmoreal Washington Obelisk,
gazing into the too long reflecting pool,
the reddish trees, the withering autumn sky,
the remorseless, amplified harangues for peace—
lovely to lock arms, to march absurdly locked
(unlocking to keep my wet glasses from slipping)
to see the cigarette match quaking in my fingers,
then to step off like green Union Army recruits
for the first Bull Run, sped by photographers,
the notables, the girls . . . fear, glory, chaos, rout . . .
our green army staggered out on the miles-long green fields,
met by the other army, the Martian, the ape, the hero,
his new-fangled rifle, his green new steel helmet.

The March 2

Where two or three were flung together, or fifty,
mostly white-haired, or bald, or women . . . sadly
unfit to follow their dream, I sat in the sunset
shade of our Bastille, the Pentagon,
nursing leg- and arch-cramps, my cowardly,
foolhardy heart; and heard, alas, more speeches,
though the words took heart now to show how weak
we were, and right. An MP sergeant kept
repeating, "March slowly through them. Don't even brush
anyone sitting down." They tiptoed through us
in single file, and then their second wave
trampled us flat and back. Health to those who held,
health to the green steel head . . . to your kind hands
that helped me stagger to my feet, and flee.

Two Walls

[1968, MARTIN LUTHER KING'S MURDER]

Somewhere a white wall faces a white wall,
one wakes the other, the other wakes the first,
each burning with the other's borrowed splendor—
the walls, awake, are forced to go on talking,
their color looks much alike, two shadings of white,
each living in the shadow of the other.
How fine our distinctions when we cannot choose!
Don Giovanni can't stick his sword through stone,
two contracting, white stone walls—their pursuit
of happiness and his, coincident. . . .
At this point of civilization, this point of the world,
the only satisfactory companion we
can imagine is death—this morning, skin lumping in my throat,
I lie here, heavily breathing, the soul of New York.

For Robert Kennedy 1925–68

Here in my workroom, in its listlessness
of Vacancy, like the old townhouse we shut for summer,
airtight and sheeted from the sun and smog,
far from the hornet yatter of his gang—
is loneliness, a thin smoke thread of vital
air. But what will anyone teach you now?
Doom was woven in your nerves, your shirt,
woven in the great clan; they too were loyal,
and you too were loyal to them, to death.
For them like a prince, you daily left your tower
to walk through dirt in your best cloth. Untouched,
alone in my Plutarchan bubble, I miss
you, you out of Plutarch, made by hand—
forever approaching your maturity.

For Eugene McCarthy

[JULY 1968]

I love you so. . . . Gone? Who will swear you wouldn't
have done good to the country, that fulfillment wouldn't
have done good to you—the father, as Freud says:
you? We've so little faith that anyone
ever makes anything better . . . the same and less—
ambition only makes the ambitious great.
The state lifts us, we cannot raise the state. . . . All
was yours though, lining down the balls for hours,
freedom of the hollow bowling-alley,
the thundered strikes, the boys. . . . Picking a quarrel
with you is like picking the petals of the daisy—
the game, the passing crowds, the rapid young
still brand your hand with sunflecks . . . coldly willing
to smash the ball past those who bought the park.

The Nihilist as Hero

"All our French poets can turn an inspired line;
who has written six passable in sequence?"
said Valéry. That was a happy day for Satan. . . .
I want words meat-hooked from the living steer,
but a cold flame of tinfoil licks the metal log,
beautiful unchanging fire of childhood
betraying a monotony of vision. . . .
Life by definition breeds on change,
each season we scrap new cars and wars and women.
But sometimes when I am ill or delicate,
the pinched flame of my match turns unchanging green,
a cornstalk in green tails and seeded tassel. . . .
A nihilist wants to live in the world as is,
and yet gaze the everlasting hills to rubble.

Reading Myself

Like thousands, I took just pride and more than just,
struck matches that brought my blood to a boil;
I memorized the tricks to set the river on fire—
somehow never wrote something to go back to.
Can I suppose I am finished with wax flowers
and have earned my grass on the minor slopes of Parnassus. . . .
No honeycomb is built without a bee
adding circle to circle, cell to cell,
the wax and honey of a mausoleum—
this round dome proves its maker is alive;
the corpse of the insect lives embalmed in honey,
prays that its perishable work live long
enough for the sweet-tooth bear to desecrate—
this open book . . . my open coffin.

Death and the Bridge

[FROM A LANDSCAPE BY FRANK PARKER]

Death gallops on a bridge of red railties and girder,
a onetime view of Boston humps the saltmarsh;
it is handpainted: this the eternal, provincial
city Dante saw as Florence and hell. . . .
On weekends even, the local TV station's
garbage disposer starts to sing at daybreak:
keep Sunday clean. We owe the Lord that much;
from the first, God squared His socialistic conscience,
gave universal capital punishment.
The red scaffolding relaxes and almost breathes:
no man is ever too good to die. . . .
We will follow our skeletons on the girder,
out of life and Boston, singing with Freud:
"God's ways are dark and very seldom pleasant."

Ice

Iced over soon; it's nothing; we're used to sickness;
too little perspiration in the bucket—
in the beginning, polio once a summer. Not now;
each day the cork more sweetly leaves the bottle,
except a sudden falseness in the breath. . . .
Sooner or later the chalk wears out the smile,
and angrily we skate on blacker ice,
playthings of the current and cold fish—
the naught is no longer asset or disadvantage,
our life too long for comfort and too brief
for perfection—Cro-Magnon, dinosaur . . .
the neverness of meeting nightly like surgeons'
apprentices studying their own skeletons,
old friends and mammoth flesh preserved in ice.

Nineteen Thirties

First Things

Worse things could happen, life is insecure,
child's fears mostly a fallacious dream;
days one like the other let you live:
up at seven-five, to bed at nine,
the absolving repetitions, the three meals,
the nutritive, unimaginative dayschool meal,
laughing like breathing, one night's sleep a day—
solitude is the reward for sickness:
leafless, dusty February trees,
the field fretted in your window, all one cloth—
your mother harrowed by child gaiety. . . .
I remember that first desertion with fear;
something made so much of me lose ground,
the irregular and certain flight to art.

First Love

Two grades above me, though two inches shorter,
Leon Straus, sixthgrade fullback, his reindeer shirt—
passion put a motor in my heart.
I pretended he lived in the house across the street.
In first love a choice is seldom and blinding:
acres of whitecaps strew that muddy swell,
old crap and white plastic jugs lodge on shore.
Later, we learn better places to cast
our saffron sperm, and grasp what wisdom fears,
breasts stacked like hawknests in her boy friend's shirt,
things a deft hand tips on its back with a stick. . . .
Is it refusal of error breaks our life—
the supreme artist, Flaubert, was a boy before
the mania for phrases enlarged his heart.

The vaporish closeness of this two-month fog;
forty summers back, my brightest summer:
the rounds of Dealer's Choice, the housebound girls,
fog, the nightlife. Then, as now, the late curfew
boom of an unknown nightbird, local hemlock
gone black as Roman cypress, the barn-garage
below the tilted Dipper lighthouse-white,
a single misanthropic frog complaining
from the water hazard on the shortest hole;
till morning! Long dreams, short nights; their faces flash
like burning shavings, scattered bait and ptomaine
caught by the gulls with groans like straining rope;
windjammer pilgrims cowled in yellow hoods,
gone like the summer in their yellow bus.

Searching

I look back to you, and cherish what I wanted:
your flashing superiority to failure,
hair of yellow oak leaves, the arrogant
tanned brunt in the snow-starch of a loosened shirt—
your bullying half-erotic rollicking. . . .
The white bluffs rise above the old rock piers,
wrecked past insuring by two hurricanes.
As a boy I climbed those scattered blocks and left
the sultry Sunday seaside crowd behind,
seeking landsend, with my bending fishing rod
a small thread slighter than the dark arc of your eyebrow. . . .
Back at school, alone and wanting you,
I scratched my four initials, R.T.S.L.
like a dirty word across my bare, blond desk.

1930's

Shake of the electric fan above our village;
oil truck, refrigerator, or just men,
nightly reloading of the village flesh—
plotting worse things than marriage. They found dates
wherever summer is, the nights of the swallow
clashing in heat, storm-signal to stay home.
At night the lit blacktop fussing like a bosom;
Court Street, Dyer Lane, School, Green, Main Street
dropping through shade-trees to the shadeless haven—
young girls are white as ever. I only know
their mothers, sweatshirts gorged with tennis balls,
still air expiring from the tilting bubble—
I too wore armor, strode riveted in cloth,
stiff, a broken clamshell labeled man.

1930's

The boys come, each year more gallant, playing chicken,
then braking to a standstill for a girl—
like bullets hitting bottles, spars and gulls,
echoing and ricocheting across the bay . . .
hardy perennials! Kneedeep in the cowpond,
far from this cockfight, cattle stop to watch us,
and having had their fill, go back to lapping
soiled water indistinguishable from heaven.
Cattle get through living, but to *live:*
Kokoschka at eighty, saying, "If you last,
you'll see your reputation die three times,
or even three cultures; young girls are always here."
They *were* there . . . two fray-winged dragonflies,
clinging to a thistle, too clean to mate.

1930'S

My legs hinge on my foreshortened bathtub
small enough for Napoleon's marching tub. . . .
The sun sallows a tired swath of balsam needles,
the color soothes, and yet the scene confines;
sun falls on so many, many other things:
Custer, leaping with his wind-gold scalplock,
half a furlong or less from the Sioux front line,
and Sitting Bull, who sent our rough riders under—
both now dead drops in the decamping mass. . . .
This wizened balsam, the sea-haze of blue gauze,
the distance plighting a tree-lip of land to the islands—
who can cash a check on solitude,
or is more loved for being distant . . . love-longing
mists my windshield, soothes the eye with milk.

Bobby Delano

The labor to breathe that younger, rawer air:
St. Mark's last football game with Groton lost on the ice-crust,
the sunlight gilding the golden polo coats
of boys with country seats on the Upper Hudson.
Why does that stale light stay? First Form hazing,
first day being sent on errands by an oldboy,
Bobby Delano, cousin of Franklin Delano Roosevelt—
deported soused off the Presidential yacht
baritoning *You're the cream in my coffee* . . .
his football, hockey, baseball letter at 15;
at 15, expelled. He dug my ass with a compass,
forced me to say "My mother is a whore."
My freshman year, he shot himself in Rio,
odious, unknowable, inspired as Ajax.

Humble in victory, chivalrous in defeat,
almost, almost. . . . I bow and watch the ashes
blush, crash, reflect: an age less privileged,
though burdened with its nobles, serfs and Faith.
The possessors. The fires men build live after them,
this night, this night, I elfin, I stonefoot,
walking the wildfire wildrose of those lawns,
filling this cottage window with the same
alluring emptiness, hearing the simmer
of the moon's mildew on the same pile of shells,
fruits of the banquet . . . boiled a brittle lobster-
shell-red, the hollow foreclaw, cracked, sucked dry,
flung on the ash-heap of a soggy carton—
two burnt-out, pinhead, black and popping eyes.

Long Summers

Months of it, and the inarticulate mist so thick
we turned invisible to one another
across the room; the floor, aslant, shot hulling
through thunderheads, gun-cotton dipped in pitch,
salmon, when lighted, as the early moon,
snuffed by the malodorous and frosted murk—
not now! Earth's solid and the sky is light,
yet even on the steadiest day, dead noon,
the sun stockstill like Joshua's in midfield,
I have to brace my hand against a wall
to keep myself from swaying—swaying wall,
straitjacket, hypodermic, helmeted
doctors, one crowd, white-smocked, in panic, hit,
stop, bury the runner on the cleated field.

Long Summers

Two in the afternoon. The restlessness.
Greek Islands. Maine. I have counted the catalogue
of ships down half its length: the blistered canvas,
the metal bowsprits, once pricking up above
the Asian outworks like a wedge of geese,
the migrant yachtsmen, and the fleet in irons. . . .
The iron bell is rocking like a baby,
the high tide's turning on its back exhausted,
the colored, dreaming, silken spinnakers
shove through the patches in the island pine,
as if vegetating millennia of lizards fed
on fern and cropped the treetops . . . a nation of gazelles,
straw-chewers in the African siesta. . . .
I never thought scorn of things; struck fear in no man.

Long Summers

Up north here, in my own country, and free—
look on it with a jaundiced eye, you'll see
the manhood of the sallowing south, *noblesse
oblige* turned redneck, and the fellaheen;
yet sometimes the Nile is wet; life's lived as painted:
those couples, one in love and profit, swaying
their children and their slaves the height of children,
supple and gentle as giraffes or newts;
the waist still willowy, and the paint still fresh;
decorum without hardness; no harness on
the woman, and no armor on the husband,
the red clay Master with his feet of clay,
catwalking lightly through his conquests, leaving
one model, dynasties of faithless copies.

1930's

The circular moon saw-wheels through the oak-grove;
below it, clouds . . . permanence of the clouds,
many as have drowned in the Atlantic.
It makes one larger to sleep with the sublime;
the Great Mother shivers under the dead oak—
such cures the bygone Reichian prophets swore to,
such did as gospel for their virgin time—
two elements were truants: man and nature.
By sunrise, the sky is nearer. Strings of fog,
such as we haven't seen in fifteen months,
catch shyly over stopping lobster boats—
smoke-dust the Chinese draftsman made eternal.
His brushwork wears; the hand decayed. A hand does—
we can have faith, at least, the hand decayed.

1930's

"After my marriage, I found myself in constant
companionship with this almost stranger I found
neither agreeable, interesting, nor admirable,
though he was always kind and irresponsible.
The first years after our one child was born,
his daddy was out at sea; that helped, I could bask
on the couch of inspiration and my dreams.
Our courtship was rough, his disembarkation
unwisely abrupt. I was animal,
healthy, easily tired; I adored luxury,
and should have been an extrovert; I usually
managed to make myself pretty comfortable. . . .
Well," she laughed, "we both were glad to dazzle.
A genius temperament should be handled with care."

Anne Dick 1. 1936

Father's letter to your father said
stiffly and much too tersely he'd been told
you visited my college rooms alone—
I can still crackle that slight note in my hand.
I see your pink father—you, the outraged daughter.
That morning nursing my dark, quiet fire
on the empty steps of the Harvard Fieldhouse in
vacation . . . saying the start of *Lycidas* to myself
fevering my mind and cooling my hot nerves—
we were nomad quicksilver and drove to Boston;
I knocked my father down. He sat on the carpet—
my mother calling from the top of the carpeted stairs,
their glass door locking behind me, no cover; you
idling in the station wagon, no retreat.

Anne Dick 2. 1936

Longer ago than I had lived till then . . .
before the *Anschluss*, the ten or twenty million
war-dead . . . but who knows now off-hand how many?
I wanted to marry you, we gazed through your narrow
bay window at the hideous concrete dome
of M.I.T., its last blanched, hectic glow
sunsetted on the bay of the Esplanade:
like the classical seaport done by Claude,
an artist more out of fashion now than Nero,
his heaven-vaulting aqueducts, swords forged from plowshares,
the fresh green knife of his unloved mother's death. . . .
The blood of our spirit dries in veins of brickdust—
Christ lost, our only king without a sword,
turning the word *forgiveness* to a sword.

Father

There was rebellion, Father, and the door was slammed.
Front doors were safe with glass then . . . you fell backward
on your heirloom-clock, the phases of the moon,
the highboy quaking to its toes. My Father . . .
I haven't lost heart to say *I knocked you down*. . . .
I have breathed the seclusion of the life-tight den,
card laid on card until the pack is used,
old Helios turning the houseplants to blondes,
moondust blowing in the prowling eye—
a parental sentence on each step misplaced. . . .
You were further from Death than I am now—
that Student ageless in her green cloud of hash,
her bed a mattress half a foot off floor . . .
as far from us as her young breasts will stretch.

Mother and Father 1

If the clock had stopped in 1936
for them, or again in '50 and '54—
they are not dead, and not until death parts us,
will I stop sucking my blood from their hurt.
They say, "I had my life when I was young."
They must have . . . dying young in middle-age;
yet often the old grow still more beautiful,
watering out the hours, biting back their tears,
as the white of the moon streams in on them unshaded;
and women too, the tanning rose, their ebb,
neither a medical, nor agricultural problem.
I struck my father; later my apology
hardly scratched the surface of his invisible
coronary . . . never to be effaced.

Mother and Father 2

This glorious oversleeping half through Sunday,
the sickroom's crimeless mortuary calm,
reprieved from leafing through the Sunday papers,
my need as a reader to think celebrities
are made for suffering, and suffer well. . . .
I remember flunking all courses but Roman history—
a kind of color-blindness made the world gray,
though a third of the globe was painted red for Britain. . . .
I think of all the ill I do and will;
love hits like the *infantile* of pre-Salk days.
I always went too far—few children can love,
or even bear their bearers, the never-forgotten
my father, *my* mother . . . these names, this function, given
by them once, given existence now by me.

Returning

If, Mother and Daddy, you were to visit us
still seeing you as beings, you'd not be welcome,
as you sat here groping the scars of the house,
spangling reminiscence with reproach,
cutting us to shades you used to skim from Freud—
that first draft lost and never to be rewritten.
No one like one's mother and father ever lived;
when I see my children, I see them only
as children, only-children like myself.
Mother and Father, I try to receive you
as if you were I, as if I were you,
trying to laugh at my old nervewracking jokes . . .
a young, unlettered couple who want to leave—
childhood, closer to me than what I love.

Mother, 1972

More than once taking both roads one night
to shake the inescapable hold of New York—
now more than before fearing everything I do
is only (only) a mix of mother and father,
no matter how unlike they were, they are—
it's not what you were or thought, but you . . .
the choked oblique joke, the weighty luxurious stretch.
Mother, we are our true selves in the bath—
a cold splash each morning, the long hot evening loll.
O dying of your cerebral hemorrhage,
lost at Rapallo, dabbing your brow a week,
bruised from stumbling to your unceasing baths,
as if you hoped to drown your killer wound—
to keep me safe a generation after your death.

Father in a Dream

We were at the faculty dining table,
Freudianizing gossip . . . not of our world;
you wore your Sunday white ducks and blue coat
seeming more in character than life.
At our end of the table, I spattered gossip,
shook salt on my wine-spill; soon we were alone,
suddenly I was talking to you alone.
Your hair, grown heavier, was peacocked out in bangs;
"I do it," you said, "to be myself . . . or younger.
I'll have to make a penny for our classes:
calc and Kipling, and catching small-mouth bass."
Age had joined us at last in the same study.
"I have never loved you so much in all my life."
You answered, "Doesn't love begin at the beginning?"

To Daddy

I think, though I don't believe it, you were my airhole,
and resigned perhaps from the Navy to be an airhole—
that Mother not warn me to put my socks on before my shoes.

Will Not Come Back

[AFTER BECQUER]

Dark swallows will doubtless come back killing
the injudicious nightflies with a clack of the beak;
but these that stopped full flight to see your beauty
and my good fortune . . . as if they knew our names—
they'll not come back. The thick lemony honeysuckle,
climbing from the earthroot to your window,
will open more beautiful blossoms to the evening;
but these . . . like dewdrops, trembling, shining, falling,
the tears of day—they'll not come back. . . .
Some other love will sound his fireword for you
and wake your heart, perhaps, from its cool sleep;
but silent, absorbed, and on his knees,
as men adore God at the altar, as I love you—
don't blind yourself, you'll not be loved like that.

Mexico

Mexico

1

The difficulties, the impossibilities . . .
I, fifty, humbled with the years' gold garbage,
dead laurel grizzling my back . . . like spines of hay;
you, some sweet, uncertain age, say twenty-seven,
untempted, unseared by honors or deception.
What help then? Not the sun, the scarlet blossom,
and the high fever of this seventh day,
the predestined diarrhea of the pilgrim,
the multiple mosquito spots, round as pesos.
Hope not for God here, or even for the gods;
the Aztecs knew the sun, the source of life,
will die, unless we feed it human blood—
we two are clocks, and only count in time . . .
the hand a knife-edge pressed against the future.

3

The lizard rusty as a leaf rubbed rough
does nothing for days but puff his throat
for oxygen . . . and tongue up passing flies,
loves only identical rusty lizards panting:
harems worthy this lord of the universe—
each thing he does generic, and not the best.
We sit on a cliff like curs, chins pressed to thumbs—
how fragrantly our cold hands warm to the live coal!
The Toltec temples pass to dust in the dusk—
the clock dial of the rising moon, dust out of time—
two clocks set back to Montezuma's fate . . .
as if we still wished to pull teeth with firetongs—
when they took a city, they murdered everything,
till the Spaniards, by reflex, finished them.

4

South of Boston, south of Washington,
south of any bearing . . . I walk the glazed moonlight:
dew on the grass and nobody about,
drawn on by my unlimited desire,
like a bull with a ring in his nose, a chain in the ring. . . .
We moved far, bull and cow, could one imagine
cattle obliviously pairing six long days:
up road and down, then up again passing the same
brick garden wall, stiff spines of hay stuck in my hide;
and always in full sight of everyone,
from the full sun to silhouetting sunset,
pinned by undimming lights of hurried cars. . . .
You're gone; I am learning to live in history.
What is history? What you cannot touch.

5

Midwinter in Cuernavaca, tall red flowers
stand up on many trees; the rock is in leaf.
The sun bakes the wallbrick large as loaves of bread—
somewhere I must have met this feverish pink
and knew its message; or is it that I've walked
you past them twenty times, and now walk back?
This stream will not flow back, not once, not twice.
I've waited, I think, a lifetime for this walk.
The white powder slides out beneath our feet,
the sterile white salt of purity; even
your puffed lace blouse is salt. The red brick glides;
bread baked for a dinner never to be served. . . .
When you left, I thought of you each hour of the day,
each minute of the hour, each second of the minute.

6

As if we chewed dry twigs and salt grasses,
filling our mouths with dust and bits of adobe,
lizards, rats and worms, we walk downhill,
love demanding we be calm, not lawful,
for laws imprison as much as they protect.
Six stone lions, allday drinkers, sit like frogs,
guarding the fountain; the three rusty arc-lights sweat;
four stone inkfish, too much sat on, bear the fountain—
no star for the guidebook . . . this city of the plain,
where the water rusts as if it bled,
and thirteen girls sit at the barroom tables,
then none, then only twenty coupled men,
homicidal with morality and lust—
devotion hikes uphill in iron shoes.

7

We're knotted together in innocence and guile;
yet we are not equal, I have lived without
sense so long the loss no longer hurts,
reflex and the ways of the world will float me free—
you, God help you, must will each breath you take . . .
The lavatory breathes sweet shocking perfume.
In Cuernavaca the night's illusory houselights
watch everyone, not just the girls, in houses
like boxes on streets where buses eat the sidewalk.
It's New Year's midnight; we three drink beer in the market
from cans garnished with salt and lime—one woman, Aztec,
sings adultery ballads, and weeps because
her husband has left her for three women—
to face the poverty all men must face at the hour of death.

8

Three pillows, end on end, rolled in a daybed
blanket—elastic, round, untroubled. For a second,
by some hallucination of my hand
I imagined I was unwrapping you. . . .
Two immovable nuns, out of habit, too fat to leave
the dormitory, have lived ten days on tea,
bouillon cubes and cookies brought from Boston.
You curl in your metal bunk-bed like my child,
I sprawl on an elbow troubled by the floor—
nuns packing, nuns ringing the circular iron stair,
nuns in pajamas scalloped through their wrappers,
nuns boiling bouillon, tea or cookies, nuns
brewing and blanketing reproval . . .
the soul groans and laughs at its lack of stature.

9

No artist perhaps, you go beyond their phrases;
you were too simple to lose yourself in words . . .
Take our last day baking on the marble veranda,
the roasting brown rock, the smoking grass, the breath
of the world risen like the ripe smoke of chestnuts,
a cleavage dropping miles to the valley's body;
and the following sick and thoughtful day,
the red flower, the hills, the valley, the Volcano—
this not the greatest thing, though great; the hours
of shivering, ache and burning, when we charged
so far beyond our courage—altitude . . .
then falling back on honest speech;
infirmity's a food the flesh must swallow,
feeding our minds . . . the mind which is also flesh.

Poor Child, you were kissed so much you thought you were
   walked on;
yet you wait in my doorway with bluebells in your hair.
Those other me's, you think, *are they meaningless in toto,*
hills coarsely eyed for a later breathless conquest,
leaving no juice in the flaw, mind lodged in mind?
A girl's not quite mortal, she asks everything. . . .
If you want to make the frozen serpent dance,
you must sing it the music of its mouth:
Sleep wastes the day lifelong behind our eyes,
night shivers at noonday in the boughs of the fir. . . .
Our conversation moved from lust to love,
asking only coolness, stillness, intercourse—
then days, days, days, days . . . how can I love you more,
short of turning into a criminal?

Eight Months Later

1. EIGHT MONTHS LATER

The flower I took away and wither and fear—
to clasp, not grasp the life, the light and fragile. . . .
It's certain we burned the grass, the grass still fumes,
the girl stands in the doorway, the red flower on the trees
where once the intermeshing limbs of Lucifer
sank to sleep on the tumuli of Lilith—
did anyone ever sleep with anyone
without thinking a split second he was God? . . .
Midsummer Manhattan—we are burnt black chips.
The worst of New York is everything is stacked,
ten buildings dance in the hat of one . . . half Europe
in half a mile. I wish we were elsewhere:
Mexico . . . Mexico? Where is Mexico?
Who will live the year back, cat on the ladder?

2. DIE GOLD ORANGEN

I see the country where the lemon blossoms,
and the pig-gold orange blows on its dark branch,
and the south wind stutters from the blue hustings;
I see it; it's behind us, love, behind us—
the bluebell is brown, the cypress points too straight—
do you see the house, the porch on marble pillars?
The sideboard is silver, and the candles blaze;
the statue stands naked to stare at you.
What have I done with us, and what was done?
And the mountain, El Volcan, a climber of clouds?
The mule-man lost his footing in the cloud,
seed of the dragon coupled in that cave. . . .
The cliff drops; over it, the water drops,
and steams out the footprints that led us on.

For Lizzie and Harriet

PART ONE

Harriet

[BORN JANUARY 4, 1957]

Half a year, then a year and a half, then
ten and a half—the pathos of a child's fractions, turn-
ing up each summer. Her God a seaslug, God a queen
with forty servants, God—you gave up . . . things whirl
in the chainsaw bite of whatever squares
the universe by name and number. For
the hundredth time, we slice the fog, and round
the village with our headlights on the ground,
like the first philosopher Thales who thought all things water.
and fell in a well . . . trying to find a car
key. . . . It can't be here, and so it must be there
behind the next crook in the road or growth
of fog—there blinded by our feeble beams,
a face, clock-white, still friendly to the earth.

Harriet

A repeating fly, blueback, thumbthick—so gross,
it seems apocalyptic in our house—
whams back and forth across the nursery bed
manned by a madhouse of stuffed animals,
not one a fighter. It is like a plane
dusting apple orchards or Arabs on the screen—
one of the mighty . . . one of the helpless. It
bumbles and bumps its brow on this and that,
making a short, unhealthy life the shorter.
I kill it, and another instant's added
to the horrifying mortmain of
ephemera: keys, drift, sea-urchin shells,
you packrat off with joy . . . a dead fly swept
under the carpet, wrinkling to fulfillment.

Elizabeth

An unaccustomed ripeness in the wood;
move but an inch and moldy splinters fall
in sawdust from the wall's aluminum paint,
once loud and fresh, now aged to weathered wood.
Squalls of the seagull's exaggerated outcry
dim out in the fog. . . . *Pace, pace.* All day our words
were rusty fish-hooks—wormwood . . . Dear Heart's-Ease,
we rest from all discussion, drinking, smoking,
pills for high blood, three pairs of glasses—soaking
in the sweat of our hard-earned supremacy,
offering a child our leathery love. We're fifty,
and free! Young, tottering on the dizzying brink
of discretion once, you wanted nothing,
but to be old, do nothing, type and think.

These Winds   (Harriet)

I see these winds, these are the tops of trees,
these are no heavier than green alder bushes;
touched by a light wind, they begin to mingle
and race for instability—too high placed
to stoop to the strife of the brush, these are the winds. . . .
Downstairs, you correct notes at the upright piano,
twice upright this midday Sunday torn from the whole
green cloth of summer; your room was once the laundry,
the loose tap beats time, you hammer the formidable
chords of *The Nocturne*, your second composition.
Since you first began to bawl and crawl
from the unbreakable lawn to this sheltered room, how often
winds have crossed the wind of inspiration—
in these too, the unreliable touch of the all.

Harriet

Spring moved to summer—the rude cold rain
hurries the ambitious, flowers and youth;
our flash-tones crackle for an hour, and then
we too follow nature, imperceptibly
change our mouse-brown to white lion's mane,
thin white fading to a freckled, knuckled skull,
bronzed by decay, by many, many suns. . . .
Child of ten, three-quarters animal,
three years from Juliet, half Juliet,
already ripened for the night on stage—
beautiful petals, what shall we hope for,
knowing one choice not two is all you're given,
health beyond the measure, dangerous
to yourself, more dangerous to others?

PART TWO

Snake

One of God's creatures, just as much as you,
or God; what other bends its back in crooks
and curves so gracefully, to yield a point;
brews a more scalding venom from cold blood;
or flings a spine-string noosed about their throats:
hysterical bird, wild pig, or screaming rabbit?
Often I see it sunning on bright, brisk days,
when the heat has ebbed from its beloved rocks;
it is seamless, scaled-down to its integrity,
coiled for indiscriminate malevolence.
Lately, its valor pushed it past man's patience;
stoned, raw-fleshed, it finds its hole—sentenced
to hibernate fifty years. . . . It will thaw, then kill—
my little whip of wisdom, lamb in wolf-skin.

Christmas Tree

Twenty or more big cloth roses, pale rose or scarlet,
coil in the branches—a winning combination
for you, who have gathered them eight years or more:
bosom-blossoms from Caribbean steambath forests,
changeless, though changed from tree to tree, from Boston to here—
transplants like you. . . . Twenty small birds or more
nip the needles; a quail, a golden warbler—
the rest not great, except for those minnowy
green things, no known species, made of woven straw:
small dangling wicker hampers to tease a cat.
A fine thing, built with love; too unconventional
for our child to buy . . . the modesty
and righteousness of a woman's ego stripped naked:
"Because I lacked ambition, men thought me mad."

Dear Sorrow

We never see him now, except at dinner,
then you quarrel, and he goes upstairs. . . .
The old playground hasn't improved its asphalt base:
no growth, two broken swings, one OK—as was!
Our half century fought to stay in place.
But my eye lies, the precinct has turned hard,
hard more like a person than a thing.
Time that mends an object lets men go,
no doctor does the work of the carpenter.
It's our nerve and ideologies die first—
then we, so thumbed, worn out, used, got by heart.
Each new day I cherish a juster perspective,
doing all for the best, and therefore doing nothing,
fired by my second alcohol, remorse.

Harriet's Dream

"The broom trees twirped by our rosewood bungalow,
not wildlife, these were tropical and straw;
the Gulf fell like a shower on the fiber-sand;
it wasn't the country like our coast of Maine—
on ice for summer. We met a couple, not people,
squares asking Father if he was his name—
none ever said that I was Harriet. . . .
They were laying beach-fires with scarlet sticks and hatchets,
our little bungalow was burning—it
had burned, I was in it. I couldn't laugh,
I was afraid when the ceiling crashed in scarlet;
the shots were boom, the fire was fizz. . . . While sleeping
I scrubbed away my scars and blisters, unable
to answer if I had ever hurt."

Left Out of Vacation

"Some fathers may have some consideration,
but he is so wonderfully eccentric,
drinking buttermilk and wearing red socks.
It was OK—not having him in Florida;
Florence is different, Mother—big deal, two girls
eating alone in the Italian restaurant!" . . .
Only God could destroy the wonders He makes,
and shelve you too among them, Charles Sumner Lowell,
shiny horsechestnut-colored Burmese Cat,
waggling your literary haunches like Turgenev,
our animal whose only friends are persons—
now boarded with cats in a cathouse, moved at random
by the universal Love that moves the stars
forever rehearsing for the perfect comeback.

Das ewig Weibliche

Birds have a finer body and tinier brain—
who asks the swallows to do drudgery,
clean, cook, pick up a peck of dust per diem?
If we knock on their homes, they wince uptight with fear,
farting about all morning past their young,
small as wasps fuming in their ash-leaf ball.
Nature lives off the life that comes to hand—
if we could feel and softly touch their being,
wasp, bee and swallow might live with us like cats.
The boiling yellow-jacket in her sack
of felon-stripe cut short above the knee
sings home . . . nerve-wrung creatures, wasp, bee and bird,
guerrillas by day then keepers of the cell,
my wife in her wooden crib of seed and feed. . . .

Our Twentieth Wedding Anniversary
(Elizabeth)

Leaves espaliered jade on our barn's loft window,
sky stretched on a two-pane sash . . . it doesn't open:
stab of roofdrip, this leaf, that leaf twings,
an assault the heartless leaf rejects.
The picture is too perfect for our lives:
in Chardin's stills, the paint bleeds, juice is moving.
We have weathered the wet of twenty years.
Many cripples have won their place in the race;
Immanuel Kant remained unmarried and sane,
no one could Byronize his walk to class.
Often the player outdistances the game. . . .
This week is our first this summer to go unfretted;
we smell as green as the weeds that bruise the flower—
a house eats up the wood that made it.

The Hard Way   (Harriet)

Don't hate your parents, or your children will hire
unknown men to bury you at your own cost.
Child, forty years younger, will we live to see
your destiny written by our hands rewritten,
your adolescence snap the feathered barb,
the phosphorescence of your wake?
Under the stars, one sleeps, is free from household,
tufts of grass and dust and tufts of grass—
night oriented to the star of youth.
I only learn from error; till lately I trusted
in the practice of my hand. In backward Maine,
ice goes in season to the tropical,
then the mash freezes back to ice, and then
the ice is broken by another wave.

Words for Muffin, a Guinea-Pig

"Of late they leave the light on in my entry,
so I won't scare, though I never scare in the dark;
I bless this arrow that flies from wall to window . . .
five years and a nightlight given me to breathe—
Heidegger said spare time is ecstasy. . . .
I am not scared, although my life was short;
my sickly breathing sounded like dry leather.
Mrs. Muffin! It clicks. I had my day.
You'll paint me like Cromwell with all my warts:
small mop with a tumor and eyes too popped for thought.
I was a rhinoceros when jumped by my sons.
I ate and bred, and then I only ate,
my life zenithed in the Lyndon Johnson 'sixties . . .
this short pound God threw on the scales, found wanting."

End of Camp Alamoosook   (Harriet)

Less than a score, the dregs of the last day,
counselors and campers squat waiting for the ferry—
the unexpected, the exotic, the early
morning sunlight is more like premature twilight:
last day of the day, foreclosure of the camp.
Glare on the amber squatters, fire of fool's-gold—
like bits of colored glass, they cannot burn.
The Acadians must have gathered in such arcs;
a Winslow, our cousin, shipped them from Nova Scotia—
no malice, merely pushing his line of work,
herding guerrillas in some Morality.
The campers suspect us, and harden in their shyness,
their gruff, faint voices hardly say hello,
singing, "Do we love it? *We love it.*"

Bringing a Turtle Home

On the road to Bangor, we spotted a domed stone,
a painted turtle petrified by fear.
I picked it up. The turtle had come a long walk,
200 millennia understudy to dinosaurs,
then their survivors. A god for the out-of-power. . . .
Faster gods come to Castine, flush yachtsmen who see
hell as a city very much like New York,
these gods give a bad past and worse future to men
who never bother to set a spinnaker;
culture without cash isn't worth their spit.
The laughter on Mount Olympus was always breezy. . . .
Goodnight, little Boy, little Soldier, live,
a toy to your friend, a stone of stumbling to God—
sandpaper Turtle, scratching your pail for water.

Returning Turtle

Weeks hitting the road, one fasting in the bathtub,
raw hamburger mossing in the watery stoppage,
the room drenched with musk like kerosene—
no one shaved, and only the turtle washed.
He was so beautiful when we flipped him over:
greens, reds, yellows, fringe of the faded savage,
the last Sioux, old and worn, saying with weariness,
"Why doesn't the Great White Father put his red
children on wheels, and move us as he will?"
We drove to the Orland River, and watched the turtle
rush for water like rushing into marriage,
swimming in uncontaminated joy,
lovely the flies that fed that sleazy surface,
a turtle looking back at us, and blinking.

Growth   (Harriet)

"I'm talking the whole idea of life, and boys,
with Mother; and then the heartache, when we're fifty. . . .
You've got to call your *Notebook*, *Book of the Century*,
but it will take you a century to write,
then I will have to revise it, when you die."
Latin, Spanish, swimming half a mile,
writing a saga with a churl named Eric,
Spanish, Spanish, math and rollerskates;
a love of party dresses, but not boys;
composing something with the bells of *Boris:*
"UNTITLED, would have to be the name of it. . . ."
You grow apace, you grow too fast apace,
too soon adult; no, not adult, like us. . . .
On the telephone, they say, "We're tired, aren't you?"

The Graduate   (Elizabeth)

"Transylvania's Greek Revival Chapel
is one of the best Greek Revival things in the South;
the College's most distinguished graduate
was a naturalist, he had a French name like Audubon.
My sister Margaret, a two-bounce basketball
player and all-Southern center, came home
crying each night because of 'Happy' Chandler,
the coach, and later Governor of Kentucky.
Our great big tall hillbilly idiots keep
Kentucky pre-eminent in basketball.
And how! Still, if you are somewhat ill-born,
you feel your soul is not quite first-class. . . ."
Never such shimmering of intelligence,
though your wind was short, and you stopped smoking.

Long Summer

At dawn, the crisp goodbye of friends; at night,
enemies reunited, who tread, unmoving,
like circus poodles dancing on a ball—
something inhuman always rising on us,
punching you with embraces, holding out
a hesitant hand, unbending as a broom;
heaping the bright logs brighter, till we sweat
and shine as if anointed with hot oil:
straight alcohol, bright drops, dime-size and silver. . . .
Each day more poignantly resolved to stay,
each day more brutal, oracular and rooted,
dehydrated, and smiling in the fire,
unbandaging his tender, blood-baked foot,
hurt when he kicked aside the last dead bottle.

No Hearing

Belief in God is an inclination to listen,
but as we grow older and our freedom hardens,
we hardly even want to hear ourselves . . .
the silent universe our auditor—
I am to myself, and my trouble sings.
The Penobscot silvers to Bangor, the annual V
of geese beats above the moonborne bay—
their flight is too certain. Dante found this path
even before his first young leaves turned green;
exile gave seniority to his youth. . . .
White clapboards, black window, white clapboards, black
    window, white clapboards—
my house is empty. In our yard, the grass straggles. . . .
I stand face to face with lost Love—my breath
is life, the rough, the smooth, the bright, the drear.

No Hearing

Discovering, discovering trees light up green at night,
braking headlights-down, ransacking the roadsides
for someone strolling, fleeing to her wide goal;
passing blanks, the white Unitarian Church,
my barn on its bulwark, two allday padlocked shacks,
the town pool drained, the old lighthouse unplugged—
I watch the muddy breakers bleach to beerfroth,
our steamer, THE STATE OF MAINE, an iceberg at drydock.
Your question, my questioner? It is for you—
crouched in the gelid drip of the pine in our garden,
invisible almost when found, till I toss a white raincoat
over your sky-black, blood-trim quilted stormcoat—
you saying *I would prefer not*, like Bartleby:
small deer trembly and steel in your wet nest!

Outlivers   (Harriet and Elizabeth)

"If we could reverse the world to what it changed
a hundred years ago, or even fifty,
scrupulous drudgery, sailpower, hand-made wars;
God might give us His right to live forever
despite the eroding miracle of science. . . ."
"Was everything that much grander than it is?"
"Nothing seems admirable until it fails;
but it's only people we should miss.
The Goth, retarded epochs like crab and clam,
wept, as we do, for his dead child." We talk
like roommates bleeding night to dawn. You say,
"I hope, of course, you both will outlive me,
but you and Harriet are perhaps like countries
not yet ripe for self-determination."

My Heavenly Shiner   (Elizabeth)

The world atop Maine and our heads is north,
zeroes through Newfoundland to Hudson Bay:
entremets chinois et canadiens.
A world like ours will tumble on our heads,
my heavenly Shiner, think of it curving on?
You quiver on my finger like a small
minnow swimming in a crystal ball,
flittering radiance on my flittering finger.
The fish, the shining fish, they go in circles,
not one of them will make it to the Pole—
this isn't the point though, this is not the point;
think of it going on without a life—
in you, God knows, I've had the earthly life—
we were kind of religious, we thought in images.

It Did   (Elizabeth)

Luck, we've had it; our character the public's—
and yet we will ripen, ripen, know we once
did most things better, not just physical
but moral—turning in too high for love,
living twenty-four hours in one shirt or skirt,
breathless gossip, the breathless singles' service.
We could have done much worse. I hope we did
a hundred thousand things much worse! Poor *X's*,
chance went this way, that way with us here:
gain counted as loss, and loss as gain: our tideluck.
It did to live with, but finally all men worsen:
drones die of stud, the saint by staying virgin . . .
old jaw only smiles to bite the feeder;
corruption serenades the wilting tissue.

Seals

If we must live again, not us; we might
go into seals, we'd handle ourselves better:
able to dawdle, able to torpedo,
all too at home in our three elements,
ledge, water and heaven—if man could restrain his hand. . . .
We flipper the harbor, blots and patches and oilslick,
so much bluer than water, we think it sky.
Creature could face creator in this suit,
fishers of fish not men. Some other August,
the easy seal might say, "I could not sleep
last night; suddenly I could write my name. . . ."
Then all seals, preternatural like us,
would take direction, head north—their haven
green ice in a greenland never grass.

Obit

Our love will not come back on fortune's wheel—

in the end it gets us, though a man know what he'd have:
old cars, old money, old undebased pre-Lyndon
silver, no copper rubbing through . . . old wives;
I could live such a too long time with mine.
In the end, every hypochondriac is his own prophet.
Before the final coming to rest, comes the rest
of all transcendence in a mode of being, hushing
all becoming. I'm for and with myself in my otherness,
in the eternal return of earth's fairer children,
the lily, the rose, the sun on brick at dusk,
the loved, the lover, and their fear of life,
their unconquered flux, insensate oneness, painful "It was. . . ."
After loving you so much, can I forget
you for eternity, and have no other choice?

[F R O M]

The Dolphin

Fishnet

Any clear thing that blinds us with surprise,
your wandering silences and bright trouvailles,
dolphin let loose to catch the flashing fish. . . .
saying too little, then too much.
Poets die adolescents, their beat embalms them,
the archetypal voices sing offkey;
the old actor cannot read his friends,
and nevertheless he reads himself aloud,
genius hums the auditorium dead.
The line must terminate.
Yet my heart rises, I know I've gladdened a lifetime
knotting, undoing a fishnet of tarred rope;
the net will hang on the wall when the fish are eaten,
nailed like illegible bronze on the futureless future.

Window

Tops of the midnight trees move helter-skelter
to ruin, if passion can hurt the classical
in the limited window of the easel painter—
love escapes our hands. We open the curtains:
a square of white-faced houses swerving, foaming,
the swagger of the world and chalk of London.
At each turn the houses wall the path of meeting,
and yet we meet, stand taking in the storm.
Even in provincial capitals,
storms will rarely enter a human house,
the crude and homeless wet is windowed out.
We stand and hear the pummeling unpurged,
almost uneducated by the world—
the tops of the moving trees move helter-skelter.

The Serpent

In my dream, my belly is yellow, panels
of mellowing ivory, splendid and still young,
though slightly ragged from defending me.
My tan and green backscales are cool to touch.
For one who has always loved snakes, it is no loss
to change nature. My fall was elsewhere—
how often I made the woman bathe in her waters.
With daylight, I turn small, a small snake
on the river path, arrowing up the jags.
Like this, like this, as the great clock clangs round,
and the green hunter leaps from turn to turn,
a new brass bugle slung on his invisible baldric;
he is groping for trout in the private river,
wherever it opens, wherever it happens to open.

Symptoms

I fear my conscience because it makes me lie.
A dog seems to lap water from the pipes,
life-enhancing water brims my bath—
(the bag of waters or the lake of the grave . . .?)
from the palms of my feet to my wet neck—
I have no mother to lift me in her arms.
I feel my old infection, it comes once yearly:
lowered good humor, then an ominous
rise of irritable enthusiasm. . . .
Three dolphins bear our little toilet-stand,
the grin of the eyes rebukes the scowl of the lips,
they are crazy with the thirst. I soak,
examining and then examining
what I really have against myself.

Double Vision

I tie a second necktie over the first;
no one is always waiting at the door,
and fills the window . . . sometimes a Burmese cat,
or maybe my Daughter on the shell of my glasses.
I turn and see persons, my pajama top
loose-knotted on the long thin neck of a chair—
make yourself at home. The cat walks out—
or does it? The room has filled with double-shadows,
sedation doubles everything I see. . . .
You can't be here, and yet we try to talk;
somebody else is farcing in your face,
we haggle at cross-purposes an hour.
While we are talking, I am asking you,
"Where is Caroline?" And you *are* Caroline.

Records

". . . I was playing records on Sunday,
arranging all my records, and I came
on some of your voice, and started to suggest
that Harriet listen: then immediately
we both shook our heads. It was like hearing
the voice of the beloved who had died.
All this is a new feeling . . . I got the letter
this morning, the letter you wrote me Saturday.
I thought my heart would break a thousand times,
but I would rather have read it a thousand times
than the detached unreal ones you wrote before—
you doomed to know what I have known with you,
lying with someone fighting unreality—
love vanquished by his mysterious carelessness."

In the Mail

Planes, trains, lorries simmer through the garden,
the reviewer sent by God to humble me
ransacking my bags of dust for silver spoons—
he and I go on typing to go on living.
There are ways to live on words in England—
reading for trainfare, my host ruined on wine . . .
as if listening to conscience were telling the truth.
"I love you, darling, there's a black void,
as black as night without you. I long to see
your face and hear your voice, and take your hand—
I'm watching a scruffy, sealcolored woodchuck graze
on weeds, then lift his greedy snout and listen;
then back to speedy feeding. He weighs a ton,
and has your familiar human aspect munching."

Old Snapshot from Venice 1952

From the salt age, yes from the salt age,
courtesans, Christians fill the churchyard close;
that silly swelled tree is a spook with a twig for a head.
Carpaccio's Venice is as wide as the world,
Jerome and his lion lope to work unfeared. . . .
In Torcello, the stone lion I snapped behind you,
venti anni fa, still keeps his poodled hair—
wherever I move this snapshot, you have moved—
it's twenty years. The courtesans and lions
swim in Carpaccio's brewing tealeaf color.
Was he the first in the trade of painting to tell tales? . . .
You are making Boston in the sulfury a.m.,
dropping Harriet at camp, Old Love,
Eternity, You . . . a future told by tealeaves.

Fall Weekend at *Milgate*

The day says nothing, and lacks for nothing . . . God;
but it's moonshine trying to gold-cap my life,
asking fees from the things I lived and loved,
pilgrim on this hard-edge Roman road.
Your portrait is fair-faced with your honesty,
the painter, your first husband, made girls stare.
Your wall mirror, a mat of plateglass sapphire,
mirror scrolls and claspleaves, shows this face,
huge eyes and dawn-gaze, rumination unruffled,
unlearning apparently, since 1952. . . . .
I watch a feverish huddle of shivering cows;
you sit making a fishspine from a chestnut leaf.
We are at our crossroads, we are astigmatic
and stop uncomfortable, we are humanly low.

2

The soaking leaves, green yellow, hold like rubber,
longer than our eyes glued to the window can take;
none tumble in the inundating air. . . .
A weak eye sees a miracle of birth.
I'm counterclockwise . . . did we meet
last April in London, late fifties in New York?
Autumn sops on our windshield with huge green leaves;
the seasons race engines in America
burying old lumber without truce—
leaf-blight and street dye and the discard girl . . .
the lover sops gin all day to solve his puzzle.
Nature, like philosophers, has one plot,
only good for repeating what it does well:
life emerges from wood and life from life.

Milgate kept standing for four centuries,
good landlord alternating with derelict.
Most fell between. We're landlords for the weekend,
and watch October go balmy. Midday heat
draws poison from the Jacobean brick,
and invites the wilderness to our doorstep:
moles, nettles, last Sunday news, last summer's toys,
bread, cheeses, jars of honey, a felled elm
stacked like construction in the kitchen garden.
The warm day brings out wasps to share our luck,
suckers for sweets, pilots of evolution;
dozens drop in the beercans, clamber, buzz,
debating like us whether to stay and drown,
or, by losing legs and wings, take flight.

Mermaid

I have learned what I wanted from the mermaid
and her singeing conjunction of tail and grace.
Deficiency served her. What else could she do?
Failure keeps snapping up transcendence,
bubble and bullfrog boating on the surface,
belly lustily lagging three inches lowered—
the insatiable fiction of desire.
None swims with her and breathes the air.
A mermaid flattens soles and picks a trout,
knife and fork in chainsong at the spine,
weeps white rum undetectable from tears.
She kills more bottles than the ocean sinks,
and serves her winded lovers' bones in brine,
nibbled at recess in the marathon.

3

Our meetings are no longer like a screening;
I see the nose on my face is just a nose,
your *bel occhi grandi* are just eyes
in the photo of you arranged as figurehead
or mermaid on the prow of a Roman dory,
bright as the morning star or a blond starlet.
Our twin black and tin Ronson butane lighters
knock on the sheet, are what they are,
too many, and burned too many cigarettes. . . .
Night darkens without your necessary call,
it's time to turn your pictures to the wall;
your moon-eyes water and your nervous throat
gruffs my directive, "*You must go now go.*"
Contralto mermaid, and stone-deaf at will.

4

I see you as a baby killer whale,
free to walk the seven seas for game,
warmhearted with an undercoat of ice,
a nerve-wrung back . . . all muscle, youth, intention,
and skill expended on a lunge or puncture—
hoisted now from conquests and salt sea
to flipper-flapper in a public tank,
big deal for Sunday children. . . . My blind love—
on the Via Veneto, a girl
counting windows in a glass cafe,
now frowning at her menu, now counting out
neanderthals flashed like shorebait on the walk. . . .
Your stamina as *inside-right* at school
spilled the topheavy boys, and keeps you pure.

5

One wondered who would see and date you next,
and grapple for the danger of your hand.
Will money drown you? Poverty, though now
in fashion, debases women as much as wealth.
You use no scent, dab brow and lash with shoeblack,
willing to face the world without more face.
I've searched the rough black ocean for you,
and saw the turbulence drop dead for you,
always lovely, even for those who had you,
Rough Slitherer in your grotto of haphazard.
I lack manhood to finish the fishing trip.
Glad to escape beguilement and the storm,
I thank the ocean that hides the fearful mermaid—
like God, I almost doubt if you exist.

Draw

The cardtable is black, the cards are played face down,
black-backs on a black cloth; and soon by luck
I draw a card I wished to leave unchosen,
and discard the one card I had sworn to hold.
Dreams lose their color faster than cut flowers,
but I remember the number on my card,
a figure no philosopher takes to bed. . . .
Should revelation be sealed like private letters,
till all the beneficiaries are dead,
and our proper names become improper Lives?
Focus about me and a blur inside;
on walks, things nearest to me go slow motion,
obscene streetlife rushes on the wheelrim,
steel shavings from the vacillating will.

Flounder

In a day we pass from the Northern Lights
to doomsday dawns. Crowds crush to work at eight,
and walk with less cohesion than the mist;
the sky, without malice, is acid, Christmas lights
are needed to reveal the Thames. God sees—
wash me as white as the sole I ate last night,
acre of whiteness, back of Folkestone sand,
cooked and skinned and white—the heart appeased.
Soles live in depth, see not, spend not . . . eat;
their souls are camouflaged to die in dishes,
flat on their backs, the posture of forgiveness—
squinch-eyes, bubbles of bloodshot worldliness,
unable ever to turn the other cheek—
at sea, they bite like fleas whatever we toss.

Plotted

Planes arc like arrows through the highest sky,
ducks *V* the ducklings across a puckered pond;
Providence turns animals to things.
I roam from bookstore to bookstore browsing books,
I too maneuvered on a guiding string
as I execute my written plot.
I feel how Hamlet, stuck with the Revenge Play
his father wrote him, went scatological
under this clotted London sky.
Catlike on a paper parapet,
he declaimed the words his prompter fed him,
knowing convention called him forth to murder,
loss of free will and license of the stage.
Death's not an event in life, it's not lived through.

The Couple

"Twice in the past two weeks I think I met
Lizzie in the recurrent dream.
We were out walking. *What sort of street*, you ask,
fair or London? It was our own street.
What did you hear and say? We heard ourselves.
The sidewalk was two feet wide. We, arm in arm,
walked, squelching the five-point oakleaves under heel—
happily, they melted under heel.
Our manner had some intimacy in my dream.
What were you doing on this honeymoon?
Our conversation had a simple plot,
a story of a woman and a man
versifying her tragedy—
we were talking like sisters . . . you did not exist."

Artist's Model

"If it were done, twere well it were done quickly—
to quote a bromide, your vacillation
is acne." And we totter off the strewn stage,
knowing tomorrow's migraine will remind us
how drink heightened the brutal flow of elocution. . . .
We follow our script as timorously as actors,
divorced from making a choice by our need to act.
"If you woke and found an egg in your shoe,
would you feel you'd lost this argument?"
It's over, my clothes fly into your borrowed suitcase,
the good day is gone, the broken champagne glass
crashes in the ashcan . . . private whims, and illusions,
too messy for our character to survive.
I come on walking off-stage backwards.

Mermaid Emerging

The institutions of society
seldom look at a particular—
Degas's snubnosed dancer swings on high,
legging the toplights, never leaving stage,
enchanting lovers of art, discerning none.
Law fit for all fits no one like a glove. . . .
Mermaid, why are you another species?
"Because, you, I, everyone is unique."
Does anyone ever make you do anything?
"Do this, do that, do nothing; you're not chained.
I am a woman or I am a dolphin,
the only animal man really loves,
I spout the smarting waters of joy in your face—
rough-weather fish, who cuts your nets and chains."

Angling

Withdrawn to a third your size, and frowning doubts,
you stare in silence through the afterdinner,
when wine takes our liberty and loosens tongues—
fair-face, ball-eyes, profile of a child,
except your eyelashes are always blacked,
each hair colored and quickened like tying a fly.
If a word amuses you, the room includes your voice,
you are audible; none can catch you out,
your flights are covered by a laughing croak—
a flowered dress lost in the flowered wall.
I am waiting like an angler with practice and courage;
the time to cast is now, and the mouth open,
the huge smile, head and shoulders of the dolphin—
I am swallowed up alive . . . I am.

Leaf-Lace Dress

Leaf-lace, a simple intricate design—
if you were not inside it, nothing much,
bits of glinting silver on crinkled lace—
you fall perhaps metallic and as good.
Hard to work out the fact that makes you good,
whole spirit wrought from toys and nondescript,
though nothing less than the best woman in the world.
Cold the green shadows, iron the seldom sun,
harvest has worn her swelling shirt to dirt.
Agony says we cannot live in one house,
or under a common name. This was the sentence—
I have lost everything. I feel a strength,
I have walked five miles, and still desire to throw
my feet off, be asleep with you . . . asleep and young.

Late Summer at *Milgate*

An air of lateness blows through the redone bedroom,
a sweetish smell of shavings, wax and oil;
the sun in heaven enflames a sanded floor.
Age is our reconciliation with dullness,
my varnish complaining, *I will never die.*
I still remember more things than I forgo:
once it was the equivalent of everlasting
to stay loyal to my other person loved—
in the fallen apple lurked a breath of spirits,
the uninhabitable granite shone
in Maine, each rock our common gravestone. . . .
I sit with my staring wife, children . . . the dour Kent sky
a smudge of mushroom. In temperate years the grass
stays green through New Year—I, my wife, our children.

Robert Sheridan Lowell

Your midnight ambulances, the first knife-saw
of the child, feet-first, a string of tobacco tied
to your throat that won't go down, your window heaped
with brown paper bags leaking peaches and avocados,
your meals tasting like Kleenex . . . too much blood is seep-
    ing . . .
after twelve hours of labor to come out right,
in less than thirty seconds swimming the blood-flood:
Little Gingersnap Man, homoform,
flat and sore and alcoholic red,
only like us in owning to middle-age.
"If you touch him, he'll burn your fingers."
"It's his health, not fever. Why are the other babies so pallid?
His navy-blue eyes tip with his head. . . . Darling,
we have escaped our death-struggle with our lives."

Overhanging Cloud

This morning the overhanging clouds are piecrust,
milelong Luxor Temples based on rich runny ooze;
my old life settles down into the archives.
It's strange having a child today, though common,
adding our further complication to
intense fragility.
Clouds go from dull to dazzle all the morning;
we have not grown as our child did in the womb,
met Satan like Milton going blind in London;
it's enough to wake without old fears,
and watch the needle-fire of the first light
bombarding off your eyelids harmlessly.
By ten the bedroom is sultry. You have double-breathed;
we are many, our bed smells of hay.

Careless Night

So country-alone, and O so very friendly,
our heaviness lifted from us by the night . . .
we dance out into its diamond suburbia,
and see the hill-crown's unrestricted lights—
all day these encroaching neighbors are out of sight.
Huge smudge sheep in burden becloud the grass,
they swell on moonlight and weigh two hundred pounds—
hulky as you in your white sheep-coat, as nervous to gallop. . . .
The Christ-Child's drifter shepherds have left this field,
gone the shepherd's breezy too predictable pipe.
Nothing's out of earshot in this daylong night;
nothing can be human without man.
What is worse than hearing the late-born child crying—
and each morning waking up glad we wake?

Wildrose

A mongrel image for all summer, our scene at breakfast:
a bent iron fence of straggly wildrose glowing
below the sausage-rolls of new-mown hay—
Sheridan splashing in his blue balloon tire:
whatever he touches he's told not to touch
and whatever he reaches tips over on him.
Things have gone on and changed, the next oldest
daughter bleaching her hair three shades lighter with beer—
but if you're not a blonde, it doesn't work. . . .
Sleeping, the always finding you there with day,
the endless days revising our revisions—
everyone's wildrose? . . . And our golden summer
as much as such people can. When most happiest
how do I know I can keep any of us alive?

Ivana

Small-soul-pleasing, loved with condescension,
even through the cro-magnon tirades of six,
the last madness of child-gaiety
before the trouble of the world shall hit.
Being chased upstairs is still instant-heaven,
not yet your sisters' weekends of voluntary scales,
accompanying on a recorder carols
rescored by the Sisters of the Sacred Heart in Kent.
Though burned, you are hopeful, accident cannot tell you
experience is what you do not want to experience.
Is the teenager the dominant of ache?
Or flirting seniles, their conversation three noises,
their life-expectancy shorter than the martyrs?
How all ages hate another age,

and lifelong wonder what was the perfect age!

Lost Fish

My heavy step is treacherous in the shallows—
once squinting in the sugared eelgrass for game,
I saw the glass torpedo of a big fish,
power strayed from unilluminating depth,
roaming through the shallows worn to bone.
I was seven, and fished without a hook.
Luckily, Mother was still omnipotent—
a battered sky, a more denuded lake,
my heavy rapier trolling rod bent *L*,
drowned stumps, muskrat huts, my record fish,
its endless waddling outpull like a turtle. . . .
The line snapped, or my knots pulled—I am free
to reach the end of the marriage on my knees.
The mud we stirred sinks in the lap of plenty.

Sick

I wake now to find myself this long alone,
the sun struggling to renounce ascendency—
two elephants are hauling at my head.
It might have been redemptive not to have lived—
in sickness, mind and body might make a marriage
if by depression I might find perspective—
a patient almost earns the beautiful,
a castle, two cars, old polished heirloom servants,
Alka-Seltzer on his breakfast tray—
the fish for the table bunching in the fishpond.
None of us can or wants to tell the truth,
pay fees for the over-limit we caught, while floating
the lonely river to senility
to the open ending. Sometimes in sickness,

we are weak enough to enter heaven.

Foxfur

"I met Ivan in a marvelous foxfur coat,
his luxurious squalor, and wished you one . . . your grizzled
knob rising from the grizzled foxfur collar.
I long to laugh with you, gossip, catch up . . . or down;
and you will be pleased with Harriet,
in the last six months she's stopped being a child,
she says God is just another great man,
an ape with grizzled sideburns in a cage.
Will you go with us to *The Messiah*,
on December 17th, a Thursday,
and eat at the *Russian Tearoom* afterward?
You're not under inspection, just missed. . . .
I wait for your letters, tremble when I get none,
more when I do. Nothing new to say."

Plane Ticket

A virus and its hash of knobby aches—
more than ever flying seems too lofty,
the season unlucky for visiting New York,
for telephoning kisses transatlantic. . . .
The London damp comes in, its smell so fertile
trees grow in my room. I read Ford's *Saddest Story*,
his *triangle* I read as his student in Nashville.
Things that change us only change a fraction,
twenty-five years of marriage, a book of life—
a choice of endings? I have my round-trip tricket. . . .
After fifty so much joy has come,
I hardly want to hide my nakedness—
the shine and stiffness of a new suit, a feeling,
not wholly happy, of having been reborn.

Flight

If I cannot love myself, can you?
I am better company depressed. . . .
I bring myself here, almost my best friend,
a writer still free to work at home all week,
reading revisions to his gulping wife.
Born twenty years later, I might have been prepared
to alternate with cooking, and wash the baby—
I am a vacation-father . . . no plum—
flown in to New York. . . . I see the rising prospect,
the scaffold glitters, the concrete walls are white,
flying like Feininger's skyscraper yachts,
geometrical romance in the river mouth,
conical foolscap dancing in the sky . . .
the runway growing wintry and distinct.

No Messiah

Sometime I must try to write the truth,
but almost everything has fallen awry
lost in passage when we said goodbye in Rome.
Even the licence of my mind rebels,
and can find no lodging for my two lives.
Some things like death are meant to have no outcome.
I come like someone naked in my raincoat,
but only a girl is naked in a raincoat.
Planesick on New York food, I feel the old
subway reverberate through our apartment floor,
I stop in our Christmas-papered bedroom, hearing
my *Nolo*, the non-Messianic man—
drop, drop in silence, then a louder drop
echoed elsewhere by a louder drop.

Sleepless

Home for the night on my ten years' workbed,
where I asked the facing brick for words, and woke
to my conscious smile of self-incrimination,
hearing then as now the distant, panting siren,
small as a harbor boat patrolling the Hudson,
persistent cry without diminishment
or crescendo through the sleepless hours.
I hear its bland monotony, the voice
that holds, and never shortcircuits the transcendence
I fiddled for imperiously and too long.
All my friends are writers. Do I deserve
to sleep, because I gave myself the breaks,
self-seeking with persistent tenderness
rivals seldom lavish on a brother?

Christmas

All too often now your voice is too bright;
I always hear you . . . commonsense and tension . . .
waking me to myself: truth, the truth, until
things are just as if they had never been.
I can't tell the things we planned for you this Christmas.
I've written my family not to phone today,
we had to put away your photographs.
We had to. We have no choice—we, I, they? . . .
Our Christmas tree seems fallen out with nature,
shedding to a naked cone of triggered wiring.
This worst time is not unhappy, green sap
still floods the arid rind, the thorny needles
catch the drafts, as if alive—I too,
because I waver, am counted with the living.

Christmas

The tedium and déjà-vu of home
make me love it; bluer days will come
and acclimatize the Christmas gifts:
redwood bear, lemon-egg shampoo, home-movie-
projector, a fat book, sunrise-red, inscribed
to me by Lizzie, "Why don't you lose yourself
and write a play about the fall of Japan?"
Slight spirits of birds, light burdens, no grave duty
to seem universally sociable
and polite. . . . We are at home and warm,
as if we had escaped the gaping jaws—
underneath us like a submarine,
nuclear and protective like a mother,
swims the true shark, the shadow of departure.

Dolphin

My Dolphin, you only guide me by surprise,
captive as Racine, the man of craft,
drawn through his maze of iron composition
by the incomparable wandering voice of Phèdre.
When I was troubled in mind, you made for my body
caught in its hangman's-knot of sinking lines,
the glassy bowing and scraping of my will. . . .
I have sat and listened to too many
words of the collaborating muse,
and plotted perhaps too freely with my life,
not avoiding injury to others,
not avoiding injury to myself—
to ask compassion . . . this book, half fiction,
an eelnet made by man for the eel fighting—

my eyes have seen what my hand did.

Index of Titles

Index of First Lines

Index of Titles

Index of First Lines

255